Globalization and Law

GLOBALIZATION

Series Editors
Manfred B. Steger
*Illinois State University, University of Hawai'i, Manoa,
and Royal Melbourne Institute of Technology*
and
Terrell Carver
University of Bristol

"Globalization" has become *the* buzzword of our time. But what does it mean? Rather than forcing a complicated social phenomenon into a single analytical framework, this series seeks to present globalization as a multidimensional process constituted by complex, often contradictory interactions of global, regional, and local aspects of social life. Since conventional disciplinary borders and lines of demarcation are losing their old rationales in a globalizing world, authors in this series apply an interdisciplinary framework to the study of globalization. In short, the main purpose and objective of this series is to support subject-specific inquiries into the dynamics and effects of contemporary globalization and its varying impacts across, between, and within societies.

Globalization and Culture
Jan Nederveen Pieterse

Rethinking Globalism
Edited by
Manfred B. Steger

Globalization and Terrorism
Jamal R. Nassar

Globalism, Second Edition
Manfred B. Steger

Globaloney
Michael Veseth

Globalization and Law
Adam Gearey

Forthcoming in the Series

Globalization and War
Tarak Barkawi

Globalization and American Empire
Kiichi Fujiwara

Globalization and Feminist Activism
Mary Hawkesworth

Globalization and International Political Economy
Mark Rupert and M. Scott Solomon

Globalization and Labor
Dimitris Stevis and Terry Boswell

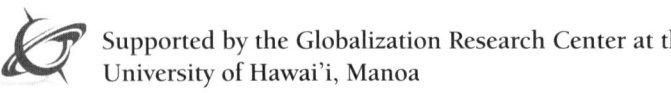

Supported by the Globalization Research Center at the University of Hawai'i, Manoa

GLOBALIZATION AND LAW

Trade, Rights, War

ADAM GEAREY

ROWMAN & LITTLEFIELD PUBLISHERS, INC.
Lanham • Boulder • New York • Toronto • Oxford

ROWMAN & LITTLEFIELD PUBLISHERS, INC.

Published in the United States of America
by Rowman & Littlefield Publishers, Inc.
A wholly owned subsidary of The Rowman & Littlefield Publishing Group,
Inc.
4501 Forbes Boulevard, Suite 200, Lanham, Maryland 20706
www.rowmanlittlefield.com

P.O. Box 317, Oxford OX2 9RU, UK

Copyright © 2005 by Rowman & Littlefield Publishers, Inc.

British Library Cataloguing in Publication Information Available

Library of Congress Cataloging-in-Publication Data

Gearey, Adam.
    Globalization and law : trade, rights, war / Adam Gearey.
        p.   cm. — (Globalization)
    Includes bibliographical references and index.
    ISBN 0-7425-3802-8 (cloth : alk. paper) — ISBN 0-7425-3803-6 (pbk. :
    alk. paper)   1. International law.   2. Globalization.   3. International
    economic relations.   4. War (International law)   5. Human rights.   I.
    Title.   II. Series: Globalization (Lanham, Md.)
KZ3410.G43   2005
341—dc22   2005009335

Printed in the United States of America

♾ ™ The paper used in this publication meets the minimum requirements of
American National Standard for Information Sciences—Permanence of Paper
for Printed Library Materials, ANSI/NISO Z39.48-1992.

CONTENTS

PREFACE

Globalization in five chapters has been a challenge. A great deal has been excluded. The only excuse I can offer is that it is an introductory book and that, ideally, it stands or falls on the extent to which it can introduce the general contours of a problematic that may be developed by further engagements with globalization. *Law and Globalization* ranges in an eclectic manner through public international law, humanitarian law, and international economic law, as well as through some aspects of private international law, human rights law, and development law. This approach is necessary as it is not possible to speak about globalization in the disciplinary boundaries that law has set for itself. Not only do these boundaries tend to obscure the complexity of the phenomena under study, but they also disassociate, or at least limit, the sense in which one can make reference to economics, politics, or international relations theory. Law tends to appear as a technical discourse, concerned with its own procedures and principles; it is an area best left to experts and those who can work its code.

We are after a style, a way of talking or thinking. As it does not yet exist, a future thinking of law and globalization would recompose the traditional legal disciplines into a broader approach, underpinned by political imperatives, and it would set out to redefine issues such as the rule of law and international justice; it would reconnect with discourses of theology and philosophy, which seem to have been stripped out of the public discourse about the subject. Against the old dogmas, it might allow us to think about our world and to argue creatively about what it might become.

This is a book of fragments, a work in progress. If it had a methodology, it would be related to Pound's "luminous method" or Rimbaud's illuminations, brief flashes of light in the darkness of the world. Obscured in the footnotes, but occasionally rising into the text, are the sparks of a thinking that owes everything to Derrida and Marx (perhaps read through Nancy): the work of fire.

Law and Globalization would have been impossible without the help of others. My first encounter with the sharp end of political economy was a visit to Gunjur in the Gambia in 1997, where my wife was working for a nongovernmental organization. Mary Gearey has helped me to think through many of the issues in this book and has labored over the manuscript with me—to her, my love and thanks. Terrell Carver has been the most inspiring of editors, his comments and advice posted from various stations of his global periplum. I would also like to thank Manfred Steger, Jennifer Kerr, and Renee Leggett for comments on the original manuscript and for their hard work. I am very grateful to all my colleagues, comrades, and friends at Birkbeck—in particular, Costas Douzinas, Fiona Macmillan, Patrick McAuslan, Michelle Everson, Peter Fitzpatrick, and Donatella Alessandrini. Thanks also to Richard Sherwin (Manhattan afternoon wandering scholarship), Peter Goodrich (vortex), Karin Van Marle, Johan Van der Walt, Dani Brant, and Wessel Le Roux (Pretoria/Johannesburg: dust and winter light).

BETWEEN THE WARS: TOWARD A JURISPRUDENCE OF THE GLOBAL

THE CLIENT: God made the world in six days, you can't make me a fucking pair of pants in six months.

THE TAILOR: But sir, take a look at the world, and then take a look at your pants.

—Samuel Beckett, *Le Monde et Le Pantalon*

Globalized law is a hybrid discourse that brings together international economy and human rights. Law is integral to the building of global institutions that are avowedly committed to international stability, sustainable world trade, and the dignity of human beings. We will thus be concerned with bodies of law that are linked with the United Nations and the other essential institutional supports of international economy: the General Agreement on Trade and Technology (GATT), the World Trade Organization (WTO), the International Monetary Fund (IMF), and the International Bank for Reconstruction and Development (hereafter, World Bank). These bodies seek to regulate the international market and to organize a global arena in which economic exchange operates to mutual advantage.[1]

We need to ask a number of critical questions. Does the global market make for the best possible generation and distribution of resources? Whose humanity lies behind the claims to human rights? Are institutions such as the World Bank transparent and dedicated to the rule of law? What is meant by *globalization*? These are the difficult issues that are addressed throughout this book.

∗   ∗   ∗

At this early stage, it is important to have a working definition of *globalization*. The term describes a complexity, a manifold of social, political, economic, and cultural forces interacting on a global scale. As a particular legal, economic, and social order, globalization has been characterized as a transition from the colonial empires of "old" Europe to an international order defined at the end of the Second World War. This era is characterized by a qualified hegemony of America and of European and Asian trade blocks. Although formal decolonization takes place in this period, the postwar world remains marked by a division between developed and developing countries.[2] Moreover, international order is defined by the foundation of powerful supranational agencies charged with the task of overseeing the operation of world economy and the protection of human rights.

Law is rooted in this political and economic complex. However, we must clarify further the kinds of law that we will focus on in this book. We will be concerned, primarily, with two bodies of law that can perhaps claim to have a global relevance: international economic law and the international law of human rights. We will also consider elements of international law, humanitarian law, and the law of war. International economic law can be understood as "the total range of norms (directly or indirectly) based on treaties of public international law with regard to transnational economic relations."[3] Within this field, our primary interest will be with the law of the IMF, the World Bank, and GATT/WTO. This means, of course, that it has been necessary to exclude a great deal. Thus, the role of transnational corporations and multinational corporations is not an explicit theme, although we will be concerned to some extent with the activities of oil companies in Nigeria and with corporate activity in the reconstruction of Iraq. Examining the law as it relates to international financial institutions can perhaps best introduce us to the difficult issues raised by globalization: in particular, the complex question of national sovereignty and the challenges for legal theory raised by bodies of law that no longer relate directly to domestic jurisdictions.

We will also concern ourselves with human rights law. Again, there

2

are problems in defining our field. A central reference point will be the Universal Declaration of Human Rights (1948), but we will also look at a major "regional" instrument: the African Charter on Human and Peoples' Rights (1981; entered into force in 1986). We will explore a particular conjunction of economics and human rights discourse in the law of development. Development law is an ongoing attempt to mend the ruptures caused by the inequitable development of global trade and financial systems. But development is itself caught up in other processes. This book moves toward an argument that wars fought for human rights are now an essential element of globalization. We will study the way in which these "humanitarian wars" demand a new understanding of the way that law operates.[4]

Globalization: Law, Economy, and Human Rights

This section is a preliminary elaboration of the themes introduced in the previous section; themes that are developed in increasing detail throughout this book. The central aim is to articulate the legal nature of those international institutions that characterize global governance and to see how they fit into a wider problematic through which economics and human rights are brought together. However, we must be careful not to suggest that this material can be neatly coordinated into a single theory of globalization; indeed, we need to gain a sense of the innate complexities of this area. As economics is perhaps the key term in describing the global, it is sensible to begin with a brief review of the arguments made for global economy. We will focus on the most recent *World Bank Report* (2001–2002) and the issue of "integration."[5] As Paul Hirst and Grahame Thompson have pointed out, in some ways the world economy is "less integrated" now than it was during the early years of the twentieth century, when the gold standard was a common reference point.[6] However, if we consider the following facts, it becomes apparent that one can speak of economic integration, even if this means no more than "when we go down, we all go together."

At the time of writing (2003), there are fears of an ongoing global recession. The *World Bank Report* describes the continuing impact of September 11, 2001, on a struggling world economy. Hardly surprisingly, the countries worst affected were developing nations hit by falling prices for commodity exports.[7] For instance, nations in the

3

Caribbean and Latin America that were relying on the export of primary products were badly affected by low coffee prices.[8] Those nations were further crippled by the reluctance of private investors to risk funds in a period of instability. In particular, foreign direct investment into the Middle East was badly hit.[9] The downturn in tourism also had negative effects. Gross domestic product (GDP) for "developing" and "transitional" countries fell from 5.4 percent in 2000 to 2.8 percent in 2001, with per capita growth falling to 1.4 percent. In East Asia and the Pacific region, growth also slowed and was further reduced by falling demand for high-tech products and by the contraction of the tourist industry. Political problems in Latin America and the Caribbean, in particular political uncertainty in Argentina, meant that the region registered the lowest growth rate, falling from 3.8 percent in 2000 to 0.6 percent in 2002.[10]

If we can tentatively accept that global integration describes international economic processes, then the next question to be addressed concerns the analysis of this phenomenon. What language can we use?[11] We also need to be able to work from a description of economy, to a characterization of the part that law plays in the global pattern. The best approach is to adopt an analytical language that has been developed in political and cultural studies. Consider the following distinction between *globalism*, *globality*, and *globalization*.[12] *Globalism* could be defined as a form of market triumphalism that ignores or downplays local politics in the new international order, a homogenization or "McDonaldization" of the planet. *Globality*, in distinction, can be understood as a rethinking of world culture in terms of difference, a mutual entanglement of different cultural traditions with a view toward their enrichment: "multiplicity without unity."[13] This could be connected with the awakenings of a global civil society and with the problems and opportunities it offers for political organization. The third term, *globalization*, describes the way in which international agencies and organizations increasingly share power with nation-states. It is said to be an irreversible process, offering opportunities to transnational corporations yet allowing a new engagement with world poverty at an international level. As the *World Bank Report* states, "Formal and informal networks have multiplied." At present, more than forty thousand treaties and five hundred multilateral agreements are registered with the UN.[14]

4

The terms *globalism* and *globalization* are employed in this study, though mutated slightly from the outline in the previous paragraph. In referring to globalized law, or law and globalization, we will be examining those normative structures that attempt to regulate economic activity. The body of law that relates to regulation of economic activities is international economic law. However, we will see that human rights law also has a role to play. Within this conjunction, national legal orders both cooperate with and offer resistance to global patterns of economic interaction. The term *globality*, while useful for cultural studies, is perhaps less of a reference point in the present work. Scholars of comparative law, anthropology, and legal history have devoted studies to the relationships between different global legal traditions, and no doubt globality may have resonance in this field. The important point to stress is that, given our focus, there is no such legal doctrinal category as globalized law. Indeed, the divisions of legal doctrine into classifications such as public international law, private international law, and human rights law make no explicit reference to globalization. We will have to look behind these traditional divisions of doctrine to observe law's response to globalization. Throughout the book, we will take an approach that stresses irresolution, engaging with legal ideas in the process of transformation. How can this be elaborated?

A starting point is to consider the attempts of governments and international organizations to "bring some order into the chaos of international trade."[15] Indeed, the desire to create a regime based on free trade and nondiscrimination remains one of the principles underlying GATT.[16] This brings us to the argument that trade tends toward the most rational and beneficial organization of resources, even though some people are disadvantaged. Originating in the works of Smith and Ricardo and given much elaboration since in the work of contemporary economists, this theory is underpinned by the principle of comparative advantage.[17] Comparative advantage theory states that in any system where there are two parties with different resources and different capacities, specialization mediated by trade leads to the greatest mutual benefit. So articulated, the theory loses a great deal of its sophistication. However, our concern is not so much to explicate this thesis but rather to locate it more broadly in a historical context. The reason is that as a structured system of international trade, it is a phenomenon bound up with the creation of the nation-state, colonialism, and the postcolonial.

   Although the idea of comparative advantage can elucidate certain aspects of world trade, we should resist a model that abstracts from material historical conditions. For instance, as argued in the following, we need to appreciate the power dynamic that runs through the operation of trade and financial systems. In the early modern period, mercantilism (in its various forms) dominated trade policy.[18] Crudely put, mercantilism tends toward a robust export policy and the creation of barriers to prevent imports. However, prompted by the British lead, free trade practices in the late nineteenth century tended to affect an increasingly global market.[19] It is worth stressing at this stage that free trade was also linked with colonialism and with the creation and perpetuation of economic inequalities. To use a phrase borrowed from the African scholar Walter Rodney, the West industrialized at the expense of the rest of the world.[20] If we concentrate on a European perspective, it could also be pointed out that "internal free trade," or the lowering of domestic tariffs, was an essential aspect of European nation building. Protectionism remained to some extent, but the aggressive British "unilateral" free trade policy encouraged free trade arrangements between other Western powers.

   Commentators suggest, however, that this period came to an abrupt end with the recessions of the 1870s and a return to protectionism (although throughout this period, U.S. trade policy alternated between protectionism and free trade).[21] Tensions created by trade policies contributed to the severe disruptions of international markets during the First World War and the protectionism that characterized the Great Depression.[22] Although there is evidence that world trade was recovering just before the outbreak of the Second World War, some economists have argued that, to avoid the destructive cycle of boom and recession, there should be some form of international trade coordination.

   High tariff bands and other restrictions on imported goods, coupled with currency devaluations, economic tensions, and recessions, contributed to the causes of the Second World War. The regulation of international trade by individual nations had thus proved to be determined by self-interest and productive of a destructive global game. After the war, the founding principles of GATT proposed a code that would create a set of rules for an "open international market."[23] GATT presents itself as a rational order based on maximalization of wealth from limited means and a legal order built on "clear" rules of conduct equally applicable to all nations.[24] There must be congruence between these orders. Indeed, the search for this coordination between law and economics characterizes much of the relevant scholarship. Within this literature there are different ways of accounting for the coherence and functioning of the "system." However, in this book, we will take an alternative approach. To present international economic law as founded on principles of rational order is itself an ideological move that obscures the way in which power relations also determine the structures of politics, society, and economy.

We have already suggested that world trade must be understood in terms of the perpetuation of relationships of dominance and subservience between developing and developed nations. This point can now be refined. Law and economics can be understood as a space of political contention and of ideological conflict,[25] where, as Manfred B. Steger has suggested, "there exists a multiplicity of stories about globalization."[26] For instance, one particularly troublesome issue is the linkage between notions of economic order and human rights. Although it can be argued that rights underpin legal systems and therefore allow the most efficient use of resources, the actuality of economic and political relations might well suggest otherwise. Unresolved tensions remain between resource management and the preservation of human dignity.

Our consideration of this issue will begin by questioning a discourse of human rights. The jurisprudence of international human rights is an expanding and dynamic area. It is impossible, in a book of this length, to cover the full range of human rights issues in any detail. Instead, we will focus on one particularly central issue: the nature of human rights. As suggested in the introduction, human rights are central to any idea of globalized law. More precisely, the era of human rights inaugurated by the foundation of the UN and the promulgation of the Universal Declaration of Human Rights in 1948 defines a body of law that is universal and hence capable of global reach.[27] There are, of course, numerous problems with this thesis, but for the moment, we will merely note its basic outline.[28] Western political thought has repeatedly returned to the notion of a just international order. Thus, the medieval Christian tradition affirmed a set of fundamental values that would bind all nations. In the succeeding early modern period, these themes were revisited and revised. Consider, for example, Kant's claim for a "perpetual peace" founded on universal, rational institutions respecting both the rights of their subjects and the rights of other states.[29] There are, of course, clear differences between the positions of Enlightenment rationalism and the claims of medieval political theologians; but to the extent that both assert overarching principles that structure world order, there is an essential similarity. The Universal Declaration of Human Rights marked a resurgence of a universal order, against the traditions that had privileged the boundaries of sovereign states and a more minimal notion of international law.

However, this familiar story of the triumph of human rights obscures a different way of reading the tradition.[30] Can a body of thought that grew largely out of Western political history provide a discourse adequate to the problems faced by the developing world? Even if we regard rights as operating strictly within a Western intellectual and political paradigm and we dismiss critiques of rights as a form of outdated political radicalism, we should at least be aware of the dynamic and antagonistic nature of human rights discourse. Consider, for a moment, the promulgation of peoples' rights during the liberation struggles against colonialism as a disruption of the "liberal" discourse of human rights. Peoples' rights were based on ideas that challenged the individualist assumptions of the dominant tradition.[31] Those engaged in liberation struggles were less accepting of existing international law norms and practices, preferring to focus on the necessary connection between law and political economy.[32] Peoples' rights were founded on the need for control over economic resources in the name of a people. Thus, there is a central linkage between the notion of a people's self-determination and the need to control the resources of a nation-state.

We need to see solidarity or peoples' rights as an essential feature of the dynamic and antagonistic nature of human rights jurisprudence. They represent an intervention into rights discourse that will take us toward the notion of a right to development. This is a particularly rich site where law, rights, and economy meet. Once again, though, we must not accord an undue coherence to a body of law that seems to be marked by tension and contestation.[33] To summarize, we need to appreciate that international economic law, human rights law, and the law of development are complex and antagonistic bodies of thought and practice. If there were one overarching concern to which we must return, it would be the extent to which there is no single discourse or theory that can describe the features of "global" law. In the following section we turn to this concern. How can we speak of jurisprudences of the global?

Legal Theory and Globalization

The themes discussed here have been considered in the existing literature on law and the challenge of globalization.[34] How can the approach in this book be compared or contrasted with the work that has been published to date? It is worth highlighting, first of all, that it has not been possible to engage with all the work done by scholars of jurisprudence in this area. What follows is an engagement with accounts that are perhaps the most controversial.

The "new" jurisprudence of the global can perhaps be best summed up by Gunther Teubner and his work in systems theory: law has become "free floating." Global law exists "without the state," no longer relying on the old logic of sovereignty. For conventional jurisprudence, sovereignty was the very foundation of law. The "maturity" of a legal system referred to its coordination with an independent political territory. Now, however, the "action" is with those bodies of international law that appear to function outside domestic boundaries and to slip out of the categories of international law, which are also predicated to a large extent on the dealings of sovereign nations. So, neither domestic law nor international law appears to provide a model for the operation of global institutions. Besides, the law is now "closely coupled with globalised socioeconomic processes." In other words, and as alluded to, global law is now escaping from the positivist assertion that law is value independent and strictly separate from politics. Global law has become politicized through its inescapable association with "highly specialized discourses" that are located in networks that run through academic, economic, and cultural sites.[35]

These claims can be elaborated by referring to *lex mercatoria*, the rules emerging from trading practices that regulate the economic dealings between merchants. *Lex mercatoria* appears to develop without a sovereign state power. This body of law has become one of the primary sites for the globalization debate within legal theory. We need to see that "private orders" (and not just states) can produce valid law.[36] *Lex mercatoria* provides a clue to an articulation of global law because it suggests that sovereignty is only one of the many ways in which nor-

mativity operates. Most controversially, a study of *lex mercatoria* suggests that rules can be rethought as acts of communication. To see rules
as acts of communication means that they are not organized on a hierarchical basis. The model of sovereignty is simply too crude. In its
place, a model of communication suggests that events are encoded as
legal or illegal, given the background assumptions and context of the
community of speakers. Merchants, taking part in trade agreements,
will make use of conventions and rules that come out of previous practices.

Why is it helpful to think of law as communication? For a start,
there are certain resonances between this idea and the notions developed within international relations theory and political theory. The fact
that the global system appears to operate beyond sovereignty has meant
that political theorists have tried to move away from more jurispruden-
tially orientated accounts of its functioning. Regime theory, for instance, articulates the operating logic of this organization as "sets of
implicit or explicit principles, norms, rules and decision making procedures around which expectations converge in a given area of international relations."[37] Indeed, this would seem helpful in describing, for
example, the code of conduct underlying GATT. It is "a mechanism
through which the political market failure that is inherent in many societies—both industrialized and developing—can be corrected, at least
in part, because reneging on liberalization commitments requires compensation for affected trading partners."[38] This suggests that the GATT
regime operates as justifier of policy and is rooted in a network of both
explicit and implicit rules that have emerged from world trade.

Although regime theory is clearly helpful, there are also problems.
Regime theory departs from any founding notion of a hierarchical
structure of norms that can be used to compel obedience and seeks instead to show how principles do indeed create obligations as well as
enable cooperation, at least if allowed to develop over time.[39] This approach helps to theorize the way that GATT and the WTO present
themselves as forums for negotiation. However, this is motivated by a
particular objective: "the exchange of liberalization commitments."[40]
This process is conceived as a benign process through which cooperation in reducing tariff barriers and other impediments to free trade will
increase efficiency and prosperity for all. Can this conception of world
trade be accepted uncritically?

Let us try to clarify our argument. It can be seen, then, that legal theory and political theory share the sense in which global regulative processes are dissimilar to domestic legal processes. Where those accounts come together, though, is in a shared assumption that sovereignty is no longer entirely sufficient to describe law and globalization. At the same time, we need to be careful. Although global processes such as trade and financial flows transcend the nation-state, there must be strong central institutions to enable the market to operate. We are concerned then with the reinscription, rather than the rejection, of sovereignty. Global space is defined both by sovereign nations and by the bodies of international economic law that operate on a somewhat different logic. We need to develop this notion of reinscription and then analyze how sovereignty and nationhood are an essential aspect of our view. However, before turning to this issue, we need to deal with some other fundamental theoretical concerns.

Perhaps systems theory overestimates the coherence of the world systems that it describes. It is certainly the case that systems theory makes use of concepts of irresolution and incongruity, but to what extent are these disturbances in the system always capable of resolution? We need to develop this theme. There is insufficient space for a general philosophical engagement with issues of contradiction and resolution, but for our purposes this is perhaps not too damaging. Compelling accounts of systemic dysfunction have been produced without recourse to an abstruse analytical vocabulary. Scholars such as MacMillan and Lowenfeld have described the lack of "congruence" between law and economics in the field of international economic law and between bodies such as the IMF and the World Bank. MacMillan has argued convincingly for a notion of "systemic disharmony," where the agendas of the World Bank, GATT, and the UN are partially supportive but tend to undermine each other.[41] This can be coordinated with the opening comments about the inchoate nature of the legal processes that we are studying, but for the moment, we need to turn to a theme that will be of immense importance for this book: the issue of power.

Given Steger's argument that globalization is a hegemonic ideology,[42] globalization needs to positioned in relation to Fitzpatrick's notion of a new legal imperialism.[43] Rules of law are themselves expressions of power relationships. It is difficult to define those words and to outline the links between them. As a working definition, though, it can

11

be suggested that power lies behind any particular conjunction of law and economics. We can treat this theme at a number of levels. The jurisprudence of international institutions rests on the preservation of particular economic relationships that are also power relationships to the extent that they concern the mobilization, deployment, and perhaps the withholding of resources. The key point is that we cannot make the mistake of seeing law as operating outside power relations. Of course, the old discourses of constitutionalism and the rule of law tend to present law in just such a manner. Law is what restrains the executive; law is strictly outside the operation of political power. Law is neutral. Scholars have pointed out the naïveté of this analysis, and we need to avoid transferring these errors to the study of global law. To align global law with a notion of legal imperialism is to see legal relations as existing in a complex conjuncture with other political, social, and cultural relations that are generally concerned with sustaining the privileged position of the developed world. Legal imperialism thus describes a new way in which power organizes itself.

Fitzpatrick's work builds on Hardt and Negri's approach to empire. Whereas the old forms of imperial empire were largely created by nations acting alone, the new legal imperialism takes shape through "institutions of the community of nations"[44] presenting themselves as an expression of global humanity. As we will see, though, these international bodies are, to some extent, greatly influenced by the developed nations that have made the greater contributions to their funds. This is to be distinguished from the structures of colonialism. The old forms of imperialism were founded on claims to territoriality, and the vast areas that were colonized by the European powers were seen as spaces to be brought within the control of the metropolitan states. Old European imperialism was profoundly hierarchical and exclusionary.[45] Against this inflexible form of conquest, the new empire is "decentred" and "deterritorialised."[46] It can be imagined as a series of capital flows and command networks that are not restricted by the limitations of a nation-state and that operate in such a way as to include and encode the world.[47] Power is horizontally organized and places actors in an ever-expanding normative network; any resistances are understood as opportunities to redesign the system so as to better organize its functioning, which is directed toward "peace" and "equilibrium"—toward more perfect regulation. Within this system, force, when necessary, is presented as being in the interests of peace and, hence, better regulation of the relations between nation-states: "the expansion of Empire is rooted in the internal trajectory of the conflicts it is meant to resolve."

There is a great deal of useful insight in this analysis. It is coherent with a pervasive theme in the broader literature.[48] Furthermore, there is an element of agreement between the systems theory that we studied earlier and this critical account of the new empire. It allows us to think of power as cohering in institutions and in the very structure of normativity. Power operates through inclusion, through classification; power is subtle and flexible, not simply the command of the rule maker. In other words, this reinscription of the notion of power is coherent with the critique of sovereignty.[49] This approach does not see power merely as the expression of sovereign or executive will or might. Power is much broader than the ability to pass law codes or to enforce them by putting tanks on the streets. Power operates at the level of the institution and its perpetuation. Indeed, in its most extended form, this theory might present the social as no more than an expression of power. It builds on Marx's insights but does not see all social relationships in terms of class interest. As a theory of global power, it describes the operation of a complex system dedicated to its own reproduction.

We need to defend the account of new imperialism from problems inherent in Hardt and Negri's analysis. Hardt and Negri do not analyze in depth the WTO, the World Bank, or GATT. We can appreciate that to some extent power is more "disembodied" than in the colonial period, but to what extent does this theory allow us to think about the institutions of international economic law and the human rights law associated with them? These bodies of law can be understood as far more restricted, far more related to the "old order" than this theory might allow. As one scholar has suggested, what is distinctive of this international regime is "a convergence of systems of municipal law among distinct sovereign states."[50] We can see a variation of this theme if we consider the way that economic law makes use of sovereignty within the area of international debt.[51] A sovereign and independent nation is, by very virtue of its being a legal entity, a potential debtor and a subject of conditionality. So, we need to appreciate that the new imperialism operates through complexes that relocate ideas such as sovereignty within new forms of imperialism. Human rights can also be approached as manifolds of power relationships.

To explain the agonistic character of rights, we can thus make use of the traditional typology of "generations," but we need to refine and adapt this model. First-generation rights can be seen as the "classical" civil liberties (for example, freedom of speech), which developed in the eighteenth and nineteenth centuries, aimed at providing protection for the individual against the state. Their paradigmatic expression is perhaps the Declaration of the Rights of Man and the Citizen after the French Revolution in 1789. Rights and civil liberties have, since this period, become central to Western democratic political orders. Second-generation rights could be found in the Covenant on Economic, Social, and Cultural Rights attached to the Universal Declaration of Human Rights. In distinction to the first category, second-generation rights, at least from the perspective of Western legal theory, state desirable principles rather than legal duties. To this extent, they interface with power structures where certain claims are seen as part of a political, rather than legal, process. Third-generation rights go further still.[52] They can be described as "solidarity rights," or rights that can only be enjoyed collectively.[53] As argued above, this last category of rights presents certain challenges to a jurisprudence that has always considered the notion of human rights as inextricably linked to the individual. Solidarity rights are legal claims that function politically: it is hardly surprising that their articulation relates in part to the struggles against colonialism.

We can now posit a fourth generation of rights: rights that justify military intervention in the name of humanity. If the first generation of rights were the product of Western political development and a particular expression of rights that suited liberal democracy, then the second and third generations can be associated with political agitation and the liberation struggles of Third World nations. One can appreciate that the call for a new international economic order in early 1974 was based on this way of thinking about rights. The right to development can also be seen as pivotal in this struggle of jurisprudences. It is situated uncomfortably between discourses that preserve the privileges of developed nations, and the struggle to equitably restructure the operation of the world economy. To some extent, this neat typology is disturbed by the new discourses growing up around governance and the World Bank, but we will deal with these issues later on in the book. Fourth-generation rights can be linked to the response of America and other Western powers to the end of the Cold War, the concept of "police actions" in the name of world peace and a challenge to the principles of multilaterialism that have structured international relations since the end of the Second World War.

As an expression of power, this most recent manifestation is an idea of rights that justifies military intervention in the name of humanity. A right of military intervention that rests on a claim to the protection of human rights shows a particular hegemonic logic and a complex relationship with the post–Second World War settlement we have been considering. In part, this is a reworking of the terms in which the UN operates and an expression of the "war against terrorism" in the aftermath of September 11. We will appreciate that this, in turn, relates back to notions of economy and development, or rather to the justification of a particular discourse of human rights that is at present making a claim to order the global space.

So far, then, we have argued that legal theory has attempted to respond to the challenges of globalization by revising or rethinking the conventional terms of jurisprudence. However, it would be too hasty to announce that concepts such as sovereignty are no longer useful. Rather, it is an issue of reinscribing, or reworking, the meanings of these terms. It is as if global law operates within a theoretical field composed of the remains of old concepts and has, as yet, failed to coordinate or arrange those fragments into a coherent structure.[54] Arguably, concepts become coherent or "solid" to the extent that they can be aligned with the preservation or perpetuation of power relationships. We have traced the outline of this theme through ideas of the economics of empire and the agonistics of human rights. These theoretical and jurisprudential concerns are now more carefully delineated within the structure of this book.

The Wearing of the World

If there is an overarching idea about globalization running through this book, it could be tentatively sketched as follows. It may be that it is simply too soon to announce a new legal logic or a new form of globalized law. We will see that many of the legal doctrines linked with the global are characterized by uncertainty and a certain instability of their key concepts. We perhaps need to appreciate that we can only talk of "global law" to the extent that we can identify bodies of law that are not yet coherent jurisprudences, or existing bodies of law—international law or international economic law, for instance, that are suffering a degree of strain in their foundational concepts.[55] A second area of concern would be areas such as African human rights law that are evolving and developing with apparently no clear overall philosophy other than the need to respond to injustice.

In this sense, we are within the wearing of the world; bodies of thought and doctrine appear to be radically unsettled. This can be linked to some broader themes. We could suggest that this goes hand in hand with the increasing stress on the role of the state and the rule of law in discourses of development. Coherent legal structures are necessary as a means of market regulation. This concern is linked with a qualified acceptance of the necessity for the state and the need to rely on the state and its agencies. Although it is hard to generalize across the different positions that make up the discourse, it might be possible to suggest that the state is increasingly linked to a notion of legitimacy that stresses democratic governance and the preservation of human rights. Likewise, the discourse of environmentalism, central to recent developments in these fields, presupposes a state willing to assume its international obligations in relation to the protection of the environment and sustainable development. A variation on this position looks to the state as the protector of people's rights. On this view, the demands of the international community are addressed to a state that acknowledges that its legitimacy is based on the willingness to safeguard and promote the claims of the different ethnicities that make up the national territory.

We can articulate at least two related "moments" in this problematic.[56] In defining the fields of law with which we are concerned, we have an issue both with their internal coherence and with the limits that demarcate them from other doctrinal areas of concern. For instance, a rigorous demarcation between public and private international law hampers one's ability to appreciate the complex interlinking of public and private agencies in the global sphere. To create any sensible legal analysis of a term such as *conditionality*, one would have to plot a series of coincidences and tensions between the international economic law of the World Bank and the IMF, various human rights codes and bodies of national law. But our concern is not just with issues that might be described as paradigm failure or epistemology.[57] We are concerned with a logic that, to some extent, "overdetermines" those issues or at least serves to distribute a number of related and interlinked problems through the doctrines we will study. It might be possible to phrase this in a simple question: how can we conceptualize the rules of a legal system based on the need simultaneously to exclude and include?[58] How are developing nations to be included in international structures that are predicated on the perpetuation of the developed world's interests? We will pursue this question through the fields of law that we have provisionally demarcated.

The next section outlines the arguments that are developed in the remaining chapters of this book.

The Persistence of the Local

Perhaps this book amounts to no more than a discourse on sovereignty. We have seen that law and globalization are marked by the very persistence of the old logic of sovereignty. In chapter 2, we will examine this thesis in more detail, with reference to the foundation and the failure of constitutional democracy in Nigeria. Nigeria's achievement of independence in 1960 is one of the definitional moments of the postcolonial and the end of an empire. It represents the shifting of political and economic relations that characterize the emergence of the world order after the Second World War. Sovereignty was the prerequisite for Nigeria to define itself as a democratic, independent nation with control over its economic resources, resources that were to be managed for the good of the nation as a whole. However, we shall see that democracy was compromised; indeed, in the face of ethnic tensions, corruption, and military dictatorships propped up by multinational corporations, sovereignty became no more than the command of whoever had been successful in the last coup. The vast revenues derived from the exploitation of oil reserves were squandered, filtered through networks of patronage or stolen by corrupt officials. However, in looking at Nigerian jurisprudence, we will see that the democratic promise of the independent nation has been sustained through a form of political legal theory.

Our concern with Nigerian politics will take us to an engagement with the fate of the Ogoni people. An ethnic minority living in the delta region of the nation, the Ogoni have found themselves the victims of the collapse of democracy. Postindependence, the Ogoni suffered the fate of being incorporated into the multiethnic Rivers State. However, the Ogoni had no representation in the federal government, no amenities, no federal investment, and no job opportunities. Since the discovery of oil on Ogoni land in 1958, the situation has worsened. Oil revenue amounts to $40 billion in Naira (N$40 billion), or US$30 billion, but the Ogoni have remained marginalized. Alongside their cultural and economic exclusion is the destruction wrought upon Ogoni land by the oil industry itself that has led to pollution and land shortages.

These issues were brought to a head by the promulgation of an Ogoni Bill of Rights and the execution of the writer Ken Saro-Wiwa and other Ogoni activists by the Nigerian state. The Ogoni Bill of Rights shows that the Ogoni were looking to the law of human rights to reinvent Nigerian democracy and the very idea of the Nigerian nation. The African Commission on Human and Peoples' Rights has taken up these demands. The local has been transformed into a much broader discourse about the failure and possibilities of African politics—in particular, the claims that citizens may have over the resources that are being exploited by the state and multinational corporations. Globalization, in this sense, is the reinvigoration of a struggle for democracy at a local level through the use of rights as limits on the activities of international business and the imposition of strict legal duties on a national government.

International Economic Law

In chapter 3, we will turn to consider international economic law as it relates to the IMF, the World Bank, and GATT/WTO. When we consider the foundational articles of these bodies, we shall see that, unlike domestic legal systems, they are largely flexible and policy oriented. Understanding their remit demands recourse to institutional history and economic objectives rather than to the autonomous legal order of a constitutional structure.

The chapter shows how a combination of hard and soft law produces the regulation of international economy. Hard law describes the imposition of enforceable legal duties and obligations. Soft law can be understood as a network of principles and policies. Whereas the former preserves a system of checks and balances in a formal division between executive, judicial, and legislative functions, the latter tends to blur those functions and to locate them within the same institution. We will see that international economic law defines itself through the creation of exceptions, or special policies that determine practices such as conditionality, or through the place of a developing nation in the rules of world trade.

Although one can make formal distinctions between the idea of the exception and the notion of the special case, for our purposes these will be downplayed because we need to appreciate the broader functioning of the soft law regime. Two further points can be made. The creation of the exception is not peculiar to soft law. It can also be found within hard law.[59] Our concern is thus with a broader structural issue: the special case must be brought within the functioning of the system. We also need to stress that although we can make distinctions between hard and soft law, it is essential that we see this distinction as being unified within the broader system. In this sense, international economic law is not concerned with the coherence of its operations from the view point of conventional jurisprudence. It is a regulatory structure, and as such, any distinctions that we are making must be seen as operating within this logic.

We will look at the foundational articles of the IMF and the World Bank and see how they have informed the development of their practices. When we turn to GATT and the WTO, we will find different but related issues. It is as if the sheer practical complexity of GATT has prevented any serious reflection on the more jurisprudential considerations that have attended its creation and early years of existence. However, we will work through our concerns with hard and soft law to show that GATT, and later the WTO, redefine law as an element within a negotiating process rather than as the command of a sovereign body.

Development Law and the Right to Development

Chapter 4 argues that development law is characterized by aporia. Indeed, we will counter the notion that development law has come of age, by suggesting that it remains within the ongoing throes of a more or less permanent crisis.

We will observe a number of interventions that attempt to resolve the foundational problems of development law. Development discourse, the field in which development law is located, grew up in parallel with the principles of international economic law as an attempt to find the way in which law could be applied to the economic and social development of Southern nations. The breakdown of this first phase of development confidence can be seen in the dual emergence of dependency theory and the discourse on the new international economic order (NIEO). Something was rotten in development. What was to be done? The United Nations Conference on Trade and Development announced a "new international development strategy" founded on the coreliance of the constituent parts of the world economy, a relationship of "dynamic interdependence" and "a more rational and equitable set of relationships between nations."[60]

The failure of the NIEO to make a difference produced another attempt at redefinition in development law: the articulation of a right to development. Once again, though, tensions appear at the very emergence of this principle. Indeed, concerns were expressed about the precise "substance" of the right.[61] We will also consider how discourses around sustainability and governance come out of similar tensions, before looking at how these themes play themselves out in contemporary development law. The crisis in development theory suggests that there are critical voices that cannot be silenced. After the NIEO, the demand for alternatives to the existing world order continue to make themselves heard.[62] From the perspective of critics in the developing world, the real reason for underdevelopment has not been understood. It is argued that discourses on sustainability and governance are attempts to police and control developing nations through a rhetoric of sharing resources that conceals certain crucial issues. Can a new version of development emerge from present calls for a tax on foreign exchange transactions and for new institutions to deal with the international debt crisis?

Humanity, War, and Rights

The final chapter argues that the Second Gulf War, of 2003, represents a terminal point for one discourse and practice of globalization and for the opening of another phase. It is obviously too soon to plot the consequences of this war, but we will use the conjunction between law and humanity to understand what is at stake in this most recent war for human rights.

In an attempt to comprehend the jurisprudential implications of these recent events, we will consider how the law deploys the notion of humanity. The law of war, or humanitarian law, is the body of rules and principles stemming from the Geneva and Hague conventions that apply to both combatants and noncombatants in conflict and postconflict situations. Apologists for this body of law have argued that it is founded on a notion of humanity. Thus, there have been attempts to show that different legal, social, and ethical traditions contain principles that can be codified to give a universal law of humanitarian conduct: "when different customs, ethics and philosophies are gathered for comparison, and when they are melted down, their particularities eliminated and only what is general extracted, one is left with a pure substance, which is the heritage of mankind."[63]

We will contrast this body of law with the developing jurisprudence that is focused on the right to intervene in the name of human rights. Some scholars have argued that this is already a coherent body of law. The first principle is that widescale and persistent violations of human rights—arising either from direct government actions or from the dislocations wrought by internal conflict or civil war—can justify military intervention. In those situations, the Security Council can take the necessary measures, and these may include the use of force.[64] The second principle is that the "abandonment" of victims of war or natural disaster, the "withholding" of aid, constitutes a threat to human life and peace and therefore also justifies intervention, backed by force if necessary. The third principle requires states to "lend support to international organizations" working to provide aid. Governments cannot use claims to sovereignty as a way of preventing international assistance for those in the midst of internal conflict. In a wider sense, these principles are backed up by those of liability for war crimes and for preventing the distribution of relief. It does not necessarily matter that the international response to crises has not itself been consistent; the grounding principle remains clear: "massive human rights deprivations do constitute a threat to international peace and security either through transboundary refugee flows or spillage of internal strife across borders." In these circumstances, the use of force is justified.[65]

Against this argument for coherence, we will contend that those notions of humanitarianism and human rights exist in a complex conjuncture with a certain discourse of rights linked to "military humanism" and with a repositioning of the relative importance of human rights and sovereignty at the level of international law. It is too soon to say whether a body of humanitarian military intervention can emerge that is not somehow related to the global reach of the "coalition of the willing," who are furthering a particular version of human rights. By the same token, arguments made about the legitimacy of intervention in the name of international security and about the threat of weapons of mass destruction and terrorism gain credibility by their association with the notion of an ethical international law. For our purposes, this complex, difficult field redefines the territory where ethical choices and commitments to a jurisprudence of the global have to be made. Given the malleability of international law, a protest that intervention is against international law may not be sufficient. Critique must move outside of the law. Returning to some of the key arguments of the book, we will insist that this right is related to certain themes in international economic law and development law that show a partial understanding of the dynamics of the "humanity" in which the military operates.

The concluding section suggests that there is a need to find humanity in the silence of those for whom human rights are meant to speak.

You Have to be Strong to Announce the End Time

Working through these problems will move us beyond the law and will invoke other discourses: how can one claim to speak for humanity?[66] Is this a final gamble or the opening of a new world order, a new globalism in the name of humanity? Whose humanity? Have we reached the end of the world? Beyond the theme of the global lies at stake the very term that opened the Western tradition, the thematic of philosophy: what is it to be human; what is humanity?

To put this somewhat differently, perhaps the discourse on globalization needs a certain shift or distortion. If we look in depth at the processes that are described in this introduction, we find that they are justified by either an implicit or explicit reference to humanity. This most general and empty of terms thus acquires a certain content: the humanity of human rights; humanity as best served by the market, and the humanity in whose name aid operations and military intervention takes place. Clearly these arguments are complex, but we need to take issue with the deployment of the term *humanity* in the debates about globalization.

To rephrase this final point, we need to appreciate that the discourse of the global requires a philosophy equal to the tasks it creates, an understanding of the ruins that we inherit.[67]

Notes

1. Verloren van Themaat, *The Changing Structures of International Law* (The Hague: Martinus Nijhoff, 1981), 1.

2. It is important to resist a simple description of ideological/regional blocs or a trite division between rich and poor countries while maintaining that world economy is structured by underlying inequalities of power and wealth.

3. Van Themaat, *Changing Structures*, 9.

4. See Jan Patočka, "Wars of the Twentieth Century and the Twentieth Century as War," in *Heretical Essays in the Philosophy of History* (Chicago: Open Court, 1996), 119–39.

5. Available at www.worldbank.org/annual report/2002/overview.htm.

6. Paul Hirst and Grahame Thompson, *Globalization in Question* (Cambridge: Polity Press; Cambridge: Blackwell, 1996).

7. For instance, "export commodity prices reduced Latin America and the Caribbean's export revenue growth to 1.4 percent in 2001, after a 19 percent rise in 2000" (see www.worldbank.org/annual report/2002/chap0506.htm).

8. See www.worldbank.org/annual report/2002/chap0506.htm.

9. In the Middle East region, economic growth slowed to 3.1 percent. This was down from 4.2 percent in the previous year. Oil exporters experienced sharp declines, from 3.6 percent to 2.5 percent. A less serious decline of 0.5 percentage points was recorded for nations that had a more diverse set of exports. See www.worldbank.org/annual report/2002/chap0506.htm.

10. See www.worldbank.org/annual report/2002/chap0506.htm.

11. For a sophisticated engagement with the analytical language of globalization, see Justin Rosenberg, *The Follies of Globalisation* (London: Verso, 2000). Rosenberg's skeptical approach to globalization theory, in particular that of Anthony Giddens, can perhaps be read as an attempt to deflate some of the grander claims and return to traditions of social and political thought where the nature of global power has always been addressed. Rosenberg provides a useful formulation that could describe the approach followed in this book: "'globalisation' . . . is at first sight merely a descriptive category, denoting

either the geographical extension of social processes, or possibly, as in Giddens' definition: 'the intensification of worldwide social relationships.'" Any explanation of these processes must "fall back on some more basic social theory," or it will fall into the same error of globalization theory: offering globalization as an explanation of globalization (see Rosenberg, *Follies of Globalisation*, 2–3 and 157–65).

12. Ulrich Beck, *What Is Globalization?* trans. Patrick Camiller (Cambridge: Polity Press, 2000), 10–15, 117–27. See also, J. A. Scholte, *Globalization: A Critical Introduction* (New York: St. Martin's Press, 2000). Scholte suggests that globalization can be understood in five ways: internationalization, liberalization, universalization, Westernization/modernization, and deterritorialization (15–16). The first four meanings have already been rigorously studied and thus cannot be seen as new phenomena. Only the notion of deterritorialization qualifies as a new object of study. It is possible to appreciate how deterritorialization is linked to Scholte's notion of the superterritorial. Whether we accept Scholte's analysis or not, these terms are useful to understand elements of the law that we are studying in this book. We are, of course, dealing with international or superterritorial bodies of law.

13. Beck, *What Is Globalization?* 10.

14. World Bank, *Annual Report 2002* (Washington, D.C.: World Bank, 2002), vii.

15. John H. Jackson, *The Jurisprudence of GATT and the WTO* (Cambridge: Cambridge University Press, 1999), 2.

16. Kenneth W. Dam, *The GATT: Law and International Economic Organization* (Chicago: University of Chicago Press, 1970).

17. Ricardo's thesis has been reworked in important ways. The factor proportions hypothesis, also known as the Heckscher-Ohin theorem, first developed in the early nineteen hundreds, argues that comparative advantage depends on a nation making best use of those factors that are in abundance— labor, for example. In the 1960s, Vernon's product cycle theory expanded the theory of comparative advantage to consider the part played by research and development. One could perhaps trace a profound shift toward a consideration of those policy factors that create comparative advantage; see Michael J. Trebicock and Robert Howse, *The Regulation of International Trade* (London: Routledge, 1995), 5–7. See also, Donatella Alessandrini, "Transnational Corporations and the Doctrine of Comparative Advantage: A Critique of Free Trade Normative Assumptions," *International Trade Law Review* 1 (2005); and Alessandrini, "WTO and Current Trade Debate: An Enquiry into the Intellectual Origins of Free Trade Thought," *International Trade Law Review* 2 (2005).

18. Andreas F. Lowenfeld, *International Economic Law* (Oxford: Oxford University Press, 2002), 9.

19. Trebicock and Howse, *Regulation of International Trade*, 18.

20. Walter Rodney, *How Europe Underdeveloped Africa* (London: Bogle-L'Ouverture Publications, 1972).

21. Trebicock and Howse, *Regulation of International Trade*, 18.

22. Trebicock and Howse, *Regulation of International Trade*, 19.

23. Robert E. Hudec, *Developing Countries in the GATT Legal System* (London: Trade Policy Research Centre, 1987), 8.

24. Van Themaat, *Changing Structures*, 17.

25. The notion of ideology employed in this book is drawn from the work of Louis Althusser. There are problems with Althusser's theory of ideology, but it can suggest, in a form of shorthand, the necessary coordinates for this most disorientating of subjects. See Louis Althusser, *For Lenin* (London: Verso, 1970). As Althusser explains, ideology is a "dream" that can only be understood as a form of "residue" (33) of the day's events in the mind of the dreamer. Because it is always driven by something "external"—economy, for example—ideology is never at home for itself; always elsewhere. A strange idea. So strange that Althusser must immediately move away from this nonobject that is both a something, in that it has effects that can be observed, and a nothing: a dream. So, what would a "theory of ideology in general" (35) attempt to show? Ideology "represents" something in an "imaginary form" (36). What does it "represent"? "The imaginary relationship of individuals to their real conditions of production" (36). Ideology reflects in an imaginary form, a "real" world (38). The crucial distinction: ideology does not reflect a real world; it is an "imaginary" relation to "real relations" (39). What is the sense of this distinction? Instead of the notion that ideology is a veil that separates the real from the unreal, it becomes the very "point" or a "hinge" that connects the subject to the real world. Ideology is thus a way of describing the mechanism through which the subject is inserted into a given material reality. In its most extended form, it is a theory of the subject as "made" by material circumstance. Thus "subjective" states are not to be seen as "essences," "ideas," or "spiritual substances" but as the very complexes that attach the subject to an external world. See also, Ernesto Laclau and Chantal Mouffe, *Hegemony and Socialist Strategy* (London: Verso, 1985). On the relationships between Freud and Marx, see Slavoj Zizek, *The Sublime Object of Ideology* (London: Verso, 1989).

26. Manfred B. Steger, *Globalism: The New Market Ideology* (Lanham, Md.: Rowman & Littlefield, 2002), 79.

27. This approach to human rights is marked by a certain Eurocentricism. The promulgation of the Universal Declaration of Human Rights as inaugurating the great age of global human rights can be seen as a call answered by the announcements of rights in the African, Islamic, and other world traditions.

28. For a more detailed genealogy of human rights, see Costas Douzinas, *The End of Human Rights* (Oxford: Hart, 1999). See also, Upendra Baxi, *The Future of Human Rights* (Oxford: Oxford University Press, 2002).

29. See Immanuel Kant, *Perpetual Peace: A Philosophical Essay*, trans. M. Campbell Smith (London: Allen & Unwin, 1915), for one of the most influential developments of the notion of an international order. Contemporary elaborations of this position can be exemplified in the work of John Rawls. There is a vast literature on Rawls, and this book does not engage explicitly with the political and jurisprudential thought of Rawls or his apologists. However, Rawlsian notions do underlie the world order that Hardt and Negri identify (see note 45). See also, Norberto Bobbio, "Democracy and the International System," in *Cosmopolitan Democracy: An Agenda for a New World Order*, ed. Daniele Archibgi and David Held (Cambridge: Polity Press, 1995), 17–39. For a critique of cosmopolitanism, see Ruth Buchanan and Sundhya Pahuja, "Collaboration, Cosmopolitanism, and Complicity," *Nordic Journal of International Law* 71 (2002): 297–324.

30. See Costas Douzinas, *The End of Human Rights* (Oxford: Hart, 1999). Douzinas presents a critical genealogy of human rights that returns to the heritage of the French Revolution and the celebrated slogan freedom, equality, and fraternity. Douzinas argues that it is necessary to make use of the unstable relationship between equality and freedom. Whereas freedom can be co-opted by those who seek to maximize their own at the expense of others, equality is less easily captured. What has to be stressed is the irreducibility of equality to freedom. The term *equality* can be traced from the Stoics through to the early Christians. It may prove easy to limit the idea to a form, but equality runs ahead of itself and gives birth to new ideas and practices that better realize its spirit. Fraternity echoes with the same tensions. It can be reduced to an anodyne notion, or it can remain challenging and difficult—as in Christ's command to love your neighbor as yourself. The adoption of the terms by those on the radical fringes of the French Revolution and by those that lay claim to their legacy displays similar tensions. It is true that equality can be limited to mean no more than equality before the law or, given a religious determination, to describe the equality of subjection before the father; but this does not obscure the sense in which the term still describes the presence of inequality, of the differences in material wealth and opportunity. This is why equality could never become a "formal expression of capitalistic interests" in the way that freedom did (164). What is so interesting about this description is a redefinition of Marxism. A great deal of ink has been split on Marx's response to the French Revolution, but here is a refounding of socialist ideals not so much on a scientific account of progress but on a disruptive relationship that exists within bourgeois ideology. Thus, equality can mark the "distinctiveness" (165) of the socialist revolution that seeks to abolish exploitation on the basis of class in the name of equality. Marx's lasting contribution is to refuse the abstractions of these terms and relate them to specific conditions, demands, and tensions within any given social order. Any contribution to the redefinition of

Marxism would have to clarify the sense in which the term has been confused and confounded by state socialists with a "crude and ascetic equalization" (166). On refigurings of Marx, see the groundbreaking text by Terrell Carver, *The Postmodern Marx* (Manchester: Manchester University Press, 1988).

31. George W. Shepherd and Mark O. C. Anikpo, eds., *Emerging Human Rights: The African Political Economy Context* (New York: Greenwood Press, 1990).

32. See Issa Shivji, *The Concept of Human Rights in Africa* (London: Codeseria, 1989).

33. For an elaboration of this theme, see William F. Fisher and Thomas Ponniah, eds., *Another World Is Possible* (London: Zed Books, 2003), esp. 309–17, on human rights: "The impact of trade liberalisation on fundamental human rights is very serious. Yet, the international legal regimes governing trade and human rights have been developed on parallel tracks, separately and sometimes inconsistently" (313).

34. To what extent has British jurisprudence, the Anglo-American canon, or the "liberal" tradition (a body of thought that begins with Bentham and includes, most notably, Austin, Hart, and Dworkin) been able to offer its intellectual resource as a thinking of globalization? This would take us toward the work of William Twining—see his *Globalisation and Legal Theory* (London: Butterworths, 2000) and his "Reviving General Jurisprudence," in *Transnational Legal Processes*, ed. Michael Likosky (London: Butterworths, 2002). We could offer some provisional comments with reference to Jeremy Bentham. It would appear, at first glance, that Bentham's approach, the great encyclopedia of legal forms, was geared to the global. The principle of utility, was also, of course, of universal application. The positing of sovereignty as the foundation of positive law is also an important aspect of this legacy. Criticized (perhaps unfairly) for a narrowness of focus on the question of law, this form of jurisprudence has seemed unattractive to those in cultural theory, politics, or sociology who have primarily driven the globalization debate. Bentham does, however, make an interesting distinction between local jurisprudence (the study of specific national jurisdiction) and universal jurisprudence (the study of the law that is common to all nations). This latter subject is narrowly defined, restricting itself to certain terms that Bentham thought should be common to all forms of law—concepts such as obligation and right, for instance. Censorial jurisprudence, on the other hand, could be prescriptive and specify the concepts and forms of organization that would be most desirable for all nations to include in their bodies of law. Bentham also created a branch of study called "international jurisprudence," concerned with relations among sovereign nations, a body of thought contrasted to the study of national legal systems. Twining's work, and that of other scholars, shows that this tradition is still vital and offers a contribution to contemporary legal theory.

35. Gunther Teubner, "Legal Pluralism in the World Society," in *Global Law without a State*, ed. Gunther Teubner (Aldershot, Eng.: Dartmouth, 1977).

36. Teubner, "Legal Pluralism," 10.

37. Bernard M. Hoekman and Michael M. Kostecki, *The Political Economy of the World Trading System* (Oxford: Oxford University Press), 2 (quoting Krasner).

38. Dam, *GATT*, 29.

39. Hoekman and Kostecki, *Political Economy*, 25.

40. Hoekman and Kostecki, *Political Economy*, 25.

41. Fiona MacMillan, *WTO and the Environment* (London: Sweet & Maxwell, 2001).

42. Steger, *Globalism*, 43–80.

43. Peter Fitzpatrick, *Modernism and the Grounds of Law* (Cambridge: Cambridge University Press, 2001), 212.

44. Fitzpatrick, *Modernism*, 212.

45. M. Hardt and A. Negri, *Empire* (Cambridge, Mass.: Harvard University Press, 2000), xii.

46. Hardt and Negri, *Empire*, xii.

47. Hardt and Negri, *Empire*, 13. The description of this new world order makes use of a kind of theoretical shorthand; the structure of world power is a "hybrid," a combination of Luhmann's system theory and Rawls's theory of justice.

48. See Gilles Deleuze and Felix Guattari, *Anti-Oedipus: Capitalism and Schizophrenia*, trans. Robert Hurley, Mark Seem, and Helen R. Lane (New York: Viking Press, 1977).

49. For a thorough elaboration of the intersections between power and sovereignty, see Stewart Motha, "The Sovereign Event in a Nation's Law," *Law and Critique* 13, no. 3 (2002): 311–38.

50. See Jarrod Wiener, *Globalization and the Harmonization of the Law* (London: Frances Pinter, 1999), 188: "the strategy of domestication and harmonization is an attempt to preserve the liberal global economy and the structure of the Westphalian system of law backed by coercive force, while arresting the negative impacts on states' public policy of international civil society."

51. International economic law has still perhaps not entirely cohered as a subject, but it is precisely this porosity that reveals an intriguing set of political and ideological difficulties in determining the subject's precise borders. There is consensus that it represents a form of public international law—see, for instance, Ignaz Seidl-Hohenveldern, *International Economic Law* (The Hague: Kluwer Law International, 1999). Seidl-Hohenveldern does not present the IMF/World Bank/GATT–WTO as central, restricting detailed analysis to "some succinct remarks on specific organisations" (85–92). However, there is a cognizance of human rights that distinguishes this book, even if the conception

of human rights is somewhat restrictive. Although the UN is seen as central, development law is not. Both Quereshi's and Lowenfeld's texts on international economic law devote attention to international financial institutions and GATT/WTO, but neither has a sense in which human rights could be an essential aspect of international economic law. Quereshi does devote a chapter to development law, and Lowenfeld certainly considers development themes; but development does not provide a category for the organization of the subject. The UN figures in both Lowenfeld and Quereshi but in different ways. Given the oppositional voices that see the UN as providing a more legitimate coordinating body for finance and trade, there is perhaps an alternative approach that would consider this theme of "reinventing" international economic law. Perhaps one of the most interesting accounts, although not a reinvention of international economic law, is Michel Belanger, *Institutions Economiques Internationales* (Paris: Economica, 1987). Although somewhat out of date, this text is organized around problematics of the NIEO and Third World debt ("Le probleme de la dette du Tiers Monde," 157). One could imagine the most perfect "anti-textbook," dedicated to showing that the subject does not cohere. For further considerations of the constitution of international economic law, see Asif Quereshi, ed., *Perspective in International Economic Law* (The Hague: Kluwer Law International, 2002). See also, Sundhya Pahuja, "Globalization and International Economic Law" in *Jurisprudence for an Interconnected Globe*, ed. Catherine Dauvergne (Dartmouth, Vt.: Ashgate Press, 2003).

52. As defined by Karel Vasek in Milan Bulajic, *Principles of International Development Law: Progressive Development of the Principles of International Law Relating to the New International Economic Order* (Dordrecht, Neth.: Martinus Nijhoff, 1986), 359.

53. See also, William H. Meyer, *Human Rights and International Political Economy in Third World Nations* (London: Praeger, 1998), 11.

54. See Scholte, *Globalization*. Scholte's work draws attention to the way in which certain phenomena resist the transformations of globalization; for instance, sovereignty survives the "superterritorial space" that globalized processes bring into being.

55. Considered in chapter 5.

56. The notion of the problematic is taken from the work of Louis Althusser; see Louis Althusser and Etienne Balibar, *Reading Capital*, trans. Ben Brewster (London: Verso, 1997). A problematic can be thought of as a theoretical field, or a field of knowledge, that defines objects in a certain manner. Within any given problematic, there is a degree of blindness to those terms that cannot be easily incorporated within a structure of knowledge. These resistances compromise any claim to provide a definitive ordering of the world. Althusser was particularly concerned to show how Marx's critique of political economy revealed the blindness of the capitalist mode of production to its own function-

ing. While not necessarily agreeing with the Althussarian project, the term *problematic* is still useful to suggest the compromised nature of any claim to completeness.

57. See the work of Thomas Khun—in particular, *The Structure of Scientific Revolutions* (Chicago: University of Chicago Press, 1970). Paradigms are "universally recognised scientific achievements that . . . provide model problems and solutions to a community of practitioners" (viii). Paradigm shifts occur when the assumptions that govern a paradigm are challenged; paradigms collapse when their foundational assumptions are no longer accepted by practitioners.

58. Jacques Derrida, *Specters of Marx* (London: Routledge, 1994).

59. Building on the work of the German jurist Carl Schmitt, Giorgio Agamben has argued that the very structure of sovereignty is determined by the articulation of the exception. Might this kind of analysis be relevant for international economic law? See Agamben, *Homo Sacer* (Stanford, Calif.: Stanford University Press, 1998.)

60. United Nations Conference on Trade and Development, "III. The Elaboration of a New International Development Strategy," report 322.

61. United Nations, *The Realization of the Right to Development* (New York: United Nations, 1991), 24.

62. "It is the responsibility of the United Nations and other public bodies to form and to communicate a convincing perception of the shared interests of all people in a secure and decent world," Friedl Weiss and Paul de Waart, "International Economic Law with a Human Face," in *International Economic Law with a Human Face*, ed. Friedl Weiss and Paul de Waart (The Hague: Kluwer, 1998), 5.

63. Jean Pictet, "Humanitarian Ideas Shared by Different Schools of Thought and Cultural Traditions," in *International Dimensions of Humanitarian Law*, Henry Dunant Institute, UNESCO (Dordrecht: Martinus Nijhoff, 1988), 4.

64. Francis Kofi Abiew, *The Evolution of the Doctrine and Practice of Humanitarian Intervention* (The Hague: Kluwer Law International, 1999), 229.

65. Abiew, *Evolution*, 230.

66. See Ian Ward, *Justice, Humanity, and the New World Order* (Aldershot, Eng.: Ashgate, 2003). For Ward, the new world order demands a new form of humanism, "a jurisprudence of compassion" that is, in part, a "public philosophy" that "balances sense and sensibility" (162). These are profound claims that deserve an extended engagement, not least around the issues of a jurisprudence as a public philosophy and the need to bring into communication emotion and reason. There are certain resonances between Ward's work and that of Shelley Wright in *International Human Rights, Decolonisation, and Globalisation*

(Routledge: London, 2001): "Human rights are not about creating a paradise on earth. I do not believe in Utopian ideals. What they do promise, and might achieve, are processes of respect and responsibility that can create the conditions necessary for humane standards of living and behaving on a global basis for all of us" (225). Wright resists any definite content for the "human" of human rights but does affirm a broader need to relate claims of humanity and humanness to their particular histories.

67. This returns us to the question of a philosophical register. See Henri Lefebvre, *De l'Etat*, vol. 4, *Les Contradictions de L'état Moderne*, collection 10/18 (Paris: Union Générale d'Editions, 1978). Lefebvre employs the expression "mondialité," or worldliness, to suggest a process that works its way through modernity. Worldliness is characterized by "the world wide market, generalizations of state power . . . unbridled demography and technology, space, the Third World and minorities, ethnic groups, women, peasants, youth, etc." As a process, it is produced by the forces of modernity but, at the same time, can conceal its own potential; as such, it is a "horizon of the possible." Thinking worldliness takes Lefebvre to Heidegger and the philosophical notion "die Welt weltet," a phrase that could perhaps be translated as "the world worlds," and suggests, for Lefebvre that "the world becomes world, becoming virtually what it was." Worldliness creates itself, it opens a horizon of possibilities. A more thorough engagement would work these ideas through to Jean Luc Nancy's texts, such as *The Sense of the World* (Minnesota: University of Minnesota Press, 1997) and *The Gravity of Thought* (New York: Humanity Books, 1993).

FRAGMENTS OUT OF THE DELUGE: NIGERIA, OIL, RIGHTS

Any reading of globalization must take into account law's association with the nation. In focusing on Nigeria, we will see that the affirmation of the local is a force associated with the postcolonial (although this involves bracketing off a Pan-Africanism that we do not have the space to study). A study of Nigeria shows that law must both affirm the general coherence of economy and nationhood with the special rights of those who, within the national territory, make a claim to protection or assistance by the state in safeguarding their own territory and belonging.

Our argument develops as follows. We need to appreciate how law in Nigeria seeks to define itself through notions of rights and nation. Our examination of this process will take us beyond conventional rights jurisprudence. Even though we can speak of an independent nation and even though we can identify a constitution and constitutional law, there is a sense in which Nigeria is yet to become a nation defined by the law. We will trace these themes through debates within Nigerian jurisprudence before turning to the economic aspects of this failure of coincidence. The two themes are then brought together with reference to the agitation for an Ogoni Bill of Rights and the state's execution of the "Ogoni Nine."

We will have to consider the problematic of a nation that must be at once universal and yet able to protect and safeguard those ethnicities that make special demands on the nation. In studying the Ogoni claims and the speech made by Saro-Wiwa before his execution, we will find that there is an alternative logic working itself out: a call for rights to come. It is necessary to appreciate that this jurisdiction is related to the African Charter on Human and Peoples' Rights and the extent to which the African Commission can develop an African jurisprudence of human rights that can include a claim to social and economic rights. In this sense, the local remains the provocation toward a general realization of the promises of the law.

Between Law and Economy: The Coming of the Nation and Its Tensions

What is a nation? Nation is a becoming: a collecting of a community of peoples with a historical and national identity.[1] As a process, it has legal, social, and economic logic. Indeed, sovereignty, the legal identifier of a nation, can be most properly conceived as the conjunction of these forces. For those developing nations that were administered as colonial territories, the process of nation building is particularly traumatic. We will consider the dynamic of the nation in the text of the Nigerian lawyer and patriot Obafemi Awolowo:

> When Britain decided to annex the territories that now constitute Nigeria, her motives were to advance her economic interests, to gain strategic military positions, and to enhance her political prestige. In order to secure these objectives it was imperative that the "natives," after having been subjugated, should be pacified. Order and law had to be maintained. Commerce does not flourish in a turbulent country, nor can military posts be maintained in a state of efficiency where the inhabitants were not amenable to orderly government.[2]

Awolowo's tract is both a blueprint for a system of national and local government, a discourse on the country's past and an imaginative engagement with its future. "Nigeria" is a country that will be brought into being by the law, but by a law that has not, as yet, been stated. At Awolowo's moment of writing in 1957, one could not talk of Nigeria as an independent nation. It was still either a convenient division of land, a line drawn on a map by Sir Charles Goldie, an administrative organization to better enable the exploitation of its resources, a collection of diverse peoples whose only common language was English. At the same time, Awolowo is invoking constitutional values and linking them to his imagination of Nigeria, simultaneously doing homage to a common law tradition and accusing it of failing, of being unable to live up to its rhetoric. Linked to this is the claim about economy:

> Every year Nigeria pays to British investors an interest of £750,000 on her national debt . . . Slavery continues in a more subtle but equally exploitative form. Not just in the servicing of the national debt, but in the ninety-nine years, during which the Mining Royalty Agreement will last, Nigeria will pay millions of pounds to the British owners of the United Africa Company Ltd.[3]

Here we have a knotting of themes. To be independent is to claim legal and economic sovereignty. Sovereignty founds a law that can recognize and give shape to the "people" in whose interest the economy will operate. Awolowo accuses the colonial power of depriving Nigeria of these essential supports of nationhood. However, once indpendence was "granted," once sovereignty was repatriated, the colonial legacy was not erased. Indeed, if we consider the Nigerian Independence Constitution 1960, we see that it was in many ways a flawed document. To build this argument, we need to examine the conjunction of failures in the political, constitutional, and economic structures of the Nigerian nation.

The Constitution

The Nigerian Independence Constitution 1960 was not "autochthonous," as it was based on a repeal of the relevant Order in Council (United Kingdom) under the Nigeria Independence Act.[4] The enactment of the 1963 constitution was also not entirely Nigerian, as the power of the enacting body rested on an act of the Westminster Parliament. Indeed, rather ominously, the only complete severance from the colonial power was to come with the coup of January 1966.[5] The Independence Constitution created a nation with bicameral federal and regional legislatures, parliamentary government, and a guarantee of fundamental rights.[6] The constitution contained a commitment to civil liberties and to the protection of the minorities that made up Nigeria's diverse political body. What became apparent, however, was the structural weakness of the center. The federal framework was distorted by the power of the regional assemblies representing local and ethnic interests. Moreover, the structure of the republic was such that the populous north could always dominate the other states that composed the federation, a tendency enshrined in the "first past the post" system of elections that had been inherited from the British political tradition.[7]

So, in speaking of the sovereign nation, we are thinking of a bounded entity, a political unity. However, at the same time that Nigerian unity is posited, it begins to unravel. We need to trace this unraveling.

The Problem of Ethnicities

The constitution first proposed was based on the federal unity of three discrete regions.[8] The regions themselves reflected the groupings of ethnic majorities. In the north, the Hausa/Fulani were the dominant grouping; the western region was controlled by the Yoruba, and the East by the Igbo. This could be called "indigenous colonialism," as the minority ethnic groups within the three regions were forced to attach themselves to the majority groupings.[9] How could this problem be solved? Regionalism vied with a set of claims that the minorities were to be best protected by the creation of a Nigerian nation in which ethnic identities were to be resolved in a broader sense of belonging. Directly before independence, however, ominous political tensions developed. Majority groups argued about who was to "lead" the country and made threats of cession. These difficulties contradicted hopes that differences could be resolved by federalism.

The civil war that broke out in 1967 was Nigeria's tragic fate. The tensions exacerbated by the British administration and suspended and deferred in the moment of independence returned to haunt the young nation.[10] Within six years of independence, the prime minister, Sir Abubakar Tafawa Balewa, was killed in a military coup led by the Igbo against Yoruba and Hausa/Fulani factions.[11] Violence bred violence, as the leader of the coup, Major-General Aguiyi-Ironsi, was in turn murdered in a second revolt, led by Hausa/Fulani generals. In the wake of violence came renewed calls for the break up of the federation; moves opposed by ethnic minority groupings. As a response to these tensions, General Ojukwu announced in May 1967 the independence of the state of Biafra, an Igbo nation. Biafra's secession was not exclusively due to ethnic tension; also lying behind the declaration of Biafran independence was the matter of oil and the possession of lucrative revenues from its exploitation. The inability to determine an equitable distribution of oil wealth that had bedeviled the drafters of the Republican Constitution (1963) thus also found its expression in the civil war.

We need to further explore this intersection of ethnicity and economy.

The Failures of Economy

The political inability to resolve ethnic tensions was exacerbated by an unbalanced economy that can also be traced back to the colonial period. Nigeria exemplifies a wider problem. Non-European nations were incorporated into patterns of trade, production, and distribution that directed resources toward the requirements of the metropolitan powers.[12]

Scholars have shown how colonialism retarded the development of Nigeria's economy. Agriculture was driven by export on terms that suited the metropolitan power, not by the need to provide for home markets and aid development. Mineral resources, likewise, were exploited for markets that existed in Europe and North America. Furthermore, the state-heavy, "extractive" structure of the economy failed to encourage entrepreneurialism.[13] An unwieldy public sector developed, rife with political placements and patronage. These economic problems can be seen as an extension of colonial policies aimed toward the development of a small, managerial elite rather than a meaningful system of democratic accountability.

The first National Development Plan (1962–1968) failed to break down this dependence on the state. The economic objectives during the period of the first republic were rapid growth and development. However, this was also in part based on structures inherited from colonialism. Continuing with "product marketing boards," policy was predicated on export of agricultural surplus to drive industrialization.

Agriculture represented 50 percent of the GDP and 75 percent of export earnings, but it was not nurtured.[14] Rather, following the theory and practice of import substitution, the key to prosperity was thought to lie in the indigenous production of consumer goods and the development of light industry. This led not to the desired goal of rapid industrial growth but to the proliferation of factories producing goods that no one could afford.[15] Moreover, the reliance on a couple of types of crops for foreign export and revenues made the economy far too sensitive to price fluctuations in those goods, a factor that also brought down foreign currency earnings and led to balance of payment problems.

These political and economic tensions were also to influence the development of the resource that would hold the key to prosperity: oil. At the time of independence, the Nigerian oil industry was largely foreign owned. It was thus similar in structure to other sectors. In the mining and tin industries foreign multinational companies also controlled productive and distributive capacity. One British-owned company, the United Africa Company, controlled over 41 percent of import and export trade.[16] There are colonial reasons for this pattern of ownership. When oil was first discovered in 1914, the Colonial Mineral Ordinance limited the availability of licenses to British companies.[17] Later Shell and BP (British Petroleum) were to reap the benefits of exclusive expropriation rights to the entire territory. Although these were much reduced by legislation after independence in 1960, Shell retained a dominant position. Shell's position was helped by the fact that the Petroleum Profits Tax Ordinance allowed an equal profit share between the Nigerian government and the company.[18] Fearing that any alteration to this agreement would damage the chances of attracting other foreign investors, the independence government continued with the precolonial agreement.

It could hardly be supposed that the former colonial power would take leave of its possessions without an eye to future economic advantage. Indeed, it might be suggested that independence was merely the logical continuation of indirect rule. Mineral rights were vested in the Crown. Here is a struggle between different laws—and another site where legal issues are wound up with economic concerns. As one commentator writes, "The corporate ownership of land by lineages remains fundamental to the traditional structure of most African societies. Therefore customary land law opposed the disruption that British rule and its new economic order occasioned. Customary law also prevented economic exploitation of the land by individual Nigerians."[19] Perhaps the Independence Constitution of 1960, in its attempt to resolve these difficulties, can be seen as a statement of legal hybridity. Taxes levied on mining would be collected by federal institutions and then distributed to the relevant regions.[20] If this situation can be conceived as a kind of legal hybrid, then its weaknesses were exploited by multinational oil companies who derived their mandate to drill from the vesting of mineral rights in the Crown. The weaknesses of the constitution meant that compensation was not forthcoming.

Oil revenues were an issue for both the federal government and foreign investors. As we have seen, deep seated political tension concerning control of the oil-rich regions led, in part, to the secession of Biafra in 1967. After the civil war, the military government continued until 1979 and oversaw the reunification and reconstruction of the country.[21] The years immediately after the war saw an increase in oil prices and in the revenues for the federal government. Driven by increasing wealth, the central government expanded to assume responsibilities that had previously fallen to the various states. National development plans were orchestrated and administered by the federal government.[22] Those centralization measures must be understood in the context of centripetal forces. As regional boundaries determined the share of the central state's beneficence, resource allocation led to political reorganizations of the country. However, tensions remained, as it was widely perceived that resource distribution was inequitably organized along ethnic lines.

Against this background, economic nationalism entrenched itself. A program of economic indigenization increased the state's share in banking, industrial, and commercial sectors.[23] A renegotiation of the licenses and agreements with foreign oil companies was accompanied by the government's increasing its shares in those foreign concerns.[24] Economic reliance on oil, and continuing failures to diversify exports meant that the economy remained sensitive to the price of oil. Furthermore, agriculture remained undeveloped; imports were not controlled; and expenditure increased dramatically as the state continued to expand the public sector. Problems were exacerbated by failures to increase production in the iron and steel industries. When the oil boom came to an end, policy abruptly began to focus on "austerity measures" and on foreign borrowings at interest rates set at a time that was not beneficial for the country.[25]

The return to civilian government after the foundation of the Second Republic in 1979 did not arrest economic decline. Indeed, one of the reasons given by the military for its coup in 1983 was the corruption and incompetence of the federal government, which had seen the GDP fall 8.5 percent between 1981 and 1983 as foreign reserves dwindled (N5.462 billion in 1980 to N798.5 million in 1983) and external debts increased (US$9 billion in 1980 to US$18 billion in 1983).[26] Oil prices continued to remain low, but the state persevered with ambitious spending projects. Attempts to develop the agricultural sector and to address the widespread and deep-seated corruption at all levels of the economy resulted in little progress, as did efforts in 1982 to achieve economic stabilization. Negotiations with the IMF also failed as the regime refused to accept the measures on which the loans were conditioned. In 1983 a coup led by General Buhari brought the end of the Second Republic. However, military rule, a ten-point plan of recovery,[27] and austerity policies failed to "overcome the economic crisis."[28]

Some have argued that the continuing failures of the Buhari regime to conduct meaningful negotiations with the IMF led to a second coup in 1985, which brought General Babangida to power. The new government was well disposed to the need for structural adjustment in the Nigerian economy, even though defaulting on loan servicing meant that it was necessary to accept "enhanced surveillance" as a condition before an aid package would be issued by the IMF and the World Bank. Characterizing this new regime was a combination of military government and a belief in the free market.[29] The objectives of the package were to impose macroeconomic discipline through control of inflation and balance of payments and to achieve a structural reorganization of the economy as a whole.[30] The necessary economic reforms allowed the military to impose "full powers of control over the economy."[31] In 1985, the military government announced a state of economic emergency.[32] Alongside the general privatization of state-controlled industries and trade liberalization, measures included compulsory savings, cuts in spending on education and health care, and the removal of subsidies on petrol and import controls. Alongside those reforms, the devaluation of the currency had a negative impact on the standard of living, as did the necessary cut backs in education and health care. These economic policies operated hand in hand with repressive measures: "the regime declared that there was no alternative to SAP [structual adjustment policies]" and "used its military force to muzzle attempts to create alternatives."[33]

The disruption and uncertainty produced by the annulment of the presidential elections and the creation of an Interim National Government in 1992 as part of the tortuous restoration to civil rule, negatively affected the economy, as did General Abacha's military coup of 1993. Abacha's regime signaled another change in direction. When Abacha took over, economic production was already in decline (GDP growth: 2.6 percent in 1993, 1 percent in 1994), and the oil industry was paralyzed by its debts and the reluctance of multinational corporations to invest in the country.[34] The industrial and manufacturing sectors were also operating well under capacity, not being aided by the negative trading conditions brought about by devaluation and the subsequent lack of foreign currency.[35] Abacha's response was to abandon the free market policies of the previous regime and resort to a form of "economic nationalism."[36] Although the currency was now pegged at an official rate, the ongoing scarcity of foreign currency and the scale and impact of black market transactions meant that currency tensions remained. The impact of this economic nationalism also meant that Nigeria's creditors were less willing to extend further facilities or reschedule existing loans. However, by 1995, Abacha's government was forced to concede and to adopt various policies proposed by the World Bank and the IMF. Economic reform was accompanied by a continuation of the repressive aspects of the previous regime. This concern takes us directly to the execution of Ken Saro-Wiwa and the Ogoni nine in 1995. But, before turning to that event, we need to assess the legal response to the political paralysis of the nation.

Tomorrow Today: Nigerian Jurisprudence as a Response to Political Crisis

Our discussion of Nigerian politics is not exhausted by the compromises or failures sketched in the previous section. There remains an optimism, a sense that potentials have not been fulfilled. Despite the number of constitutions that have been enacted, the law has yet to define the Nigerian state. Nigerian jurisprudence can be read as being organized around this key concern. Its problematic is the invention of the nation, a theme that is associated with the development of a doctrine for the rule of law that is suited to Nigerian political realities. How can one speak of the law when the state is in the hands of a military dictatorship? It is interesting that General Obasanjo, who came to power after the assassination of General Mohammed in 1976, justified his military regime in terms of the rule of law.[37] His argument was that the military had to become involved in politics to return the country to the path of constitutionalism. If one rejects this justification of dictatorship, then jurisprudence must make for a reinvention of democracy. When one legal philosopher asks whether Nigerian jurisprudence was born yesterday or today, the answer to the riddle may be that Nigerian jurisprudence awaits its rebirth.[38] If there is the sense that contemporary law in Nigeria reflects a colonial inheritance in the preservation of dictatorship, then one might say that the democratic promise of the Independence Constitution is yet to be realized. Thus the search for a Nigerian jurisprudence is simultaneously a quest for a point of legal resistance to both the legacy of colonialism and the reality of military dictatorship.

Nigerian jurisprudence can be seen as defining itself within and against the positivism of the jurist Hans Kelsen. Inherited from Kelsen's "pure" legal theory is the need to strip law of any reference to politics, history, or ideology and "indeed ethics."[39] The quest is for law's logical and, hence, most universal form. From this perspective, the relevant issue is the fundamental source of Nigerian law, or rather, the question "[What] supports the Supreme Military Council upon whose shoulders the governance of the entire country rests?"[40] There are a number of possible answers, ranging from the constitution through to the revolutionary act of violence that brought the military to power. It would represent a political and ethical failure to conclude that merely seizing power is the justifying act. The central issue for a positivist jurisprudence needs to be reassessed. Implicit in Kelsen's theory is the claim that the *Grundnorm*, or foundational norm of the constitution, commands a minimum of uncoerced support. It is necessary to identify a legal foundation that meets this criterion.

When the protectorates of Northern and Southern Nigeria were created by the British, the *Grundnorm* was the Crown in Parliament, which "would expect to be obeyed, even though most of the time [the British] were reluctantly obeyed."[41] Precisely because it was imposed through force, there could be no sense in which it enjoyed legitimacy. The 1946 constitution could be criticized for the same reasons. The Independence Constitution that established the first republic would appear to have the mark of legitimacy that is presupposed by the *Grundnorm*. However, what needed to be clarified was whether the *Grundnorm* lay with the executive or with the Supreme Court. The outcome of *Akintola v. Adegbenro* suggests that it was firmly on the side of the executive.[42] Whatever issues were left unresolved by this case and the 1963 Constitution, the coup of January 1966 placed the powers of the legislature, the executive, and the judiciary in the hands of the military council. The decision in *Lakanmi v. AG* was radical in that it declared that the courts themselves were the source of the *Grundnorm*.[43] However, Decree 28 of 1970 overturned this position and affirmed that ultimate power lie with the military. Concerns regarding ultimate authority became most acute with the fall of the Second Republic in the coup of 1983. The supremacy of the 1979 constitution, fundamental rights, and the right of civil action against acts done pursuant to a military decree were all suspended.

This search for a formal *Grundnorm* leads to this dead end. In a country driven by military coups, the whole issue of the *Grundnorm* is perhaps too restrictive a test, too narrow a concept to provide a theory of law equal to the nation. Can an approach be found in an appeal beyond law? To a notion of Nigerian history? How can this be more thoroughly elaborated?

A historical jurisprudence suggests a foundational reference to an alternative body of thought. Of late, the work of the German legal philosopher Von Savigny has been seen of increasing relevance to the Nigerian situation. Von Savigny is presented as a rival to both positivism and natural law theory. A historical school of jurisprudence can orientate study more thoroughly to the way that law develops out of a people's appreciation of their "social background." Although there is no formal definition of law in Von Savigny,[44] there is an understanding of law as "an aspect of the total common life of the nation, not something made by the nation as a matter of choice or convention, but, like its manners and language, bound up with its existence."[45] The work of Von Savigny is being drawn upon but not in a "strict Savigny-sense."[46] Adaptation to an African reality is also its jurisprudential transformation.

Von Savigny can be used, first of all, to castigate the law of the British (Ordinance 3 of 1863). Was this the law of the people? It is more properly a law dispensed by the British to facilitate their "trade" with the locals. To the extent that native law and custom were an acknowledged legal source there may be an indigenous influence, but the guiding spirit here was "imperialism."[47] The Royal Niger Company, whose founding charter gave it this power, dispensed the law. Sir James Marshall, the first chief justice of the Nigerian Province, was also a director of the company, an arrangement severely compromising any claims to justice that might be made. A review of the laws passed in the colonial period would suggest that they served the interests of the colonial state. It is only with the catalogue of fundamental human rights in the Constitution of 1960 that any movement of Nigerian law to the protection of the rights of citizens could be identified. This could only be given a real sense if the Nigerian courts sought to protect those rights against the executive and legislative arms of the state. In the landmark decision of *Olawoyin v. Commissioner of Police*,[48] the Supreme Court declared that, as the legislation was obscure, the court itself must assume "the role of legislator, since we are dealing with a case which the legislature can hardly be supposed to have considered."[49]

Developed from Von Savigny's work is the assertion that law is not just a "defence of society against violence"; there has to be the sense that law "benefits the people generally."[50] Here is a radical claim that reflects both a theory of history and a faith in a notion of a Nigerian people. What problems must this law face? How can it be defined in the tension between the local and the global? Nigerian jurisprudence is clearly making use of the democratic potential of the courts to uphold the constitution, but there are two fundamental difficulties. What should be the response of legal philosophy to the problems of ethnic tension? Given the need to develop an equitable distribution of the state's resources, how can the law develop a way of thinking that can realize this need as the point at which a nation could cohere? It may be necessary to make reference beyond history to a certain discourse of human rights to resolve this problem. Furthermore, in the face of a ruthless military government, must this jurisprudential thinking remain inchoate, utopian, able to imagine the nation under law but unable to bring it into effect?

In the next section, we will see how these themes work themselves out with reference to the Ogoni Bill of Rights and the wider context of the African Charter on Human and Peoples' Rights.

Ken Saro-Wiwa and Ogoni Rights

Although it is impossible to determine with certainty that Saro-Wiwa was a reader of legal philosophy, there is a clear sense in which his invocation of justice for the Ogoni people resonates with jurisprudential echoes. The championing of the Ogoni cause also returns to concerns of economy and just distribution. As with all counterpositions, though, Saro-Wiwa's work forces us to start again, to reread a history:

> Under the military dictatorships which have ruled the country from 1967 to [1992], the determination has been to subvert the federal culture of the country, establish a unitary state, corner the oil reserves of the nation at the center and then have these resources transferred by the Big Man who has come to power either by electoral fraud or military coup to the ethnic majority areas.[51]

The past repeats itself in the present; history is a cycle of violence. Can a point be affirmed that offers a new beginning? *Genocide in Nigeria*, the text from which these lines are taken, could be read as a reworking, a kind of continuation of the discourse ignited by Awolowo. However, the dream of a strong, unified Nigeria, "Africa's main contribution to the international sphere,"[52] is disturbed by a threat that lies at the heart of the nation. This is the division of the country into three ethnic groupings. The nation is not identified with a new, inclusive, and difficult identity; a bringing together of majority and minority groups. Government becomes an opportunity for the aggrandizement of whoever can seize the central reins of power. So, try to start again a different view of Nigeria from the perspective of the Ogoni; a different history; an attempt to confront the ethnic tensions and the failures of the law hidden by empire; a different tradition: "tradition in Ogoni means in the local tongue (doonu kuneke) the honouring of the land (earth, soil, water)."[53]

When is a nation a *nation*? Consider that an ethnic group of about five hundred thousand people settled in eastern Nigeria at the mouth of the River Niger. Their origins are uncertain. They might have crossed over from what is now Ghana; alternatively, their origins may have lain across the Imo River. They organized themselves into six kingdoms with distinctive languages and animistic beliefs. The forests that surrounded them were filled with animals whose souls were once those of humans. Central to Ogoni identity is a claim about the land. The Ogoni consider the land to be sacred, entrusted to their preservation. The cycles of the Ogoni's year link them to the seasons and the earth. Festivals celebrate the harvest and the time when crops are sown. A worldview is built on an awareness of the human rootedness in nature and the fragility of the environment.

The key to Saro-Wiwa's discourse is this countertime of contested claims. Already at the beginnings of Saro-Wiwa's account is an implicit claim about sovereignty. Law is used by both the British colonial state and the Nigerian state to deprive the Ogoni of their rights. This is also an exploitation of the economic benefits obtained from Ogoni land and expropriated by the Nigerian state. We need to trace this theme. Furthermore, we need to appreciate that it is linked to a history of a people and a place.

The recent history of the Ogoni is an account of their oppression by British power and then by a Nigerian federation dominated by majority ethnic groups. The fate of the Ogoni is bound up with the form of the nation that the British imposed. After 1914, the Ogoni were included in a structure that suited the needs of imperial power. Despite the historical autonomy of the Ogoni peoples, they were governed as part of a province.[54] However, the Ogoni proved to be particularly resistant to the Pax Britannica. Failures to establish a workable system of taxation and a functioning system of courts led in 1932 to the stationing of a British divisional officer in Ogoni territory and the construction of communications links with the rest of the country. Those changes had the effect of intensifying Ogoni claims for an autonomous region of administration.[55]

Ogoni confidence increased and was reflected in organizations that pressed for claims of self-determination in any future federal Nigerian state, claims that were forwarded by Ogoni representatives at both local and national levels. Even if the Ogoni had made advances in their political organization in this period, the tensions that attended Nigerian independence were to have a deep impact on any future claims to self-determination. The secession of Biafra was also a period of frustration. Any demands made to the Biafran government about the needs for regional self-determination were treated in the same high-handed way as they had been in the past by the Nigerian government, but now the Ogoni found themselves either made refugees as the federal forces invaded the rebel state or forcefully conscripted into the Biafran army and serving as frontline soldiers. Saro-Wiwa reports that over 10 percent of the ethnic group died in the war.[56]

The need to rebuild the state after the ravages of a three-year war meant that Ogoni territory was to be occupied by foreign oil companies acting in concert with the Nigerian government. As the laws that related to the extraction of oil were lacking in detail, Shell and BP were able to maximize their profits at the expense of the Ogoni by despoiling their land. For a people dependent on agriculture, the siting of refineries and boreholes seriously disrupted farming, and the pollution from the operations added to the destruction of environment and livelihood: "Shell BP is the Leviathan to whom we have been forced to surrender all our Rights including our LIFE."[57] The postwar situation continued the exploitation of the Ogoni by both oil companies and the Nigerian state. After the overthrow of General Gowon in 1975, the reorganization of the state structure was such that it increased the share of oil revenue claimed by the majority groups. The 1979 Constitution vested all oil and mineral rights in the federal government, and the land use decree, made part of the Constitution, specified that the same body held all land. This was a direct usurpation of the rights of any ethnic grouping to the economic resources of the land that they had historically settled and called their own.

International observers have called attention to the widespread corruption in government.[58] Those with political power and patronage could override legal regulation of the oil industry. For instance, it is reckoned that General Abacha's "presidential allocation" was one-tenth of total production, a share that was distributed among his favorites and collaborators. Foreign companies in turn relied on their "contacts" in government to give them influence in the industry, although, of course, palace coups and the replacement of favorites affected those jockeying for position. Originally the 1979 constitution specified that, before land could be compulsorily acquired, there had to be payment of compensation. However, this protection was ignored and sidelined by the military governments who either forbade the courts to examine executive acts or suspended sections of the constitution.[59] The Land Use Act of 1978 is key to the question of compensation. It vested the land of each state in the care and trust of the governor to use in the interests of "all Nigerians." It is within the governor's power to regulate "occupancy" of land and to order the payment of rent. Land can be acquired in the public interest, but the courts are not able to examine any executive decision taken in relation to the act. As the *Human Rights Watch Report* states, "Land is acquired by the oil companies for oil operations from the Nigerian government under these laws, which in practice allow the government to expropriate land for the oil industry with no effective due process protections for those whose livelihoods may be destroyed by the confiscation of their land."[60] In the face of such corruption, could the law still provide a way of restructuring Nigerian politics? A faith in the possibilities of a legal solution underlies the publication in 1985 of an Ogoni Bill of Rights, a charter that was addressed to the federal government of General Babangida.

The Ogoni Bill of Rights

Saro-Wiwa was one of the authors of the Ogoni Bill of Rights. It can be read as a document that brings historical and legal material together. The structure of the argument is focused in the following claim:

> Successive Federal administrators have trampled on every minority right enshrined in the Nigerian Constitution to the detriment of the Ogoni and have by administrative structuring and other noxious acts transferred Ogoni wealth exclusively to other parts of the Republic.[61]

The bill of rights presents itself as a renewal of democracy. The 1979 constitution contained a broad catalogue of rights and liberties that had been more honored in name than practice. The Ogoni document positions itself as a call for justice, for the reinvention of law and democracy in Nigeria. The federal government is asked to honor the promises made in the Independence Constitution. Precisely because the bill was presented to the Nigerian Parliament, it presupposes representative democracy and a state structure that can give redress. The tragedy of the bill may be that addressing such structures may be futile, given the marginalization of the Ogoni in the federal structure of Nigeria. We can read it as a manifesto of the local, a set of claims that affirm the persistence of a tradition in the face of the disruptive powers of a national government and multinational business.

The solution envisaged by the bill is the autonomy of the Ogoni. Autonomy is not conceived as separation or secession from the federal republic; the Ogoni were not concerned with political independence as such. On the contrary, they were affirming the federal ideal of Nigeria. Ogoni autonomy translates into a number of general demands. Central is the call for "political control" over their personal destiny. This means that the Ogoni must be able to command an equitable proportion of the revenues derived from the exploitation of oil and gas and to direct it toward their own development. Accompanying this is a claim for cultural autonomy and the need for protection from environmental degradation. The concluding section of the bill is worth considering in full:

> We make the above demand in the knowledge that it does not deny any other ethnic group in the Nigerian Federation of their rights and that it can only conduce to peace, justice and fair play and hence stability and progress in the Nigerian nation.[62]

This clause confounds the argument so frequently used against expressions of political localism: politics, so the argument runs, must affirm the general, the national interest. Any local interest must always be secondary. However, the Ogoni Bill of Rights navigates this tension between the local and the universal. The quoted paragraph stresses that the bill has to be located within the federation. The claims of the Ogoni are in fact no more than the realization of the truth of the federation: they seek to deny no other people their rights, merely to make a claim for "justice" or "fairness." To return to a previous point, the Ogoni Bill of Rights is a call for a renewal of democracy. It can be connected to the discussion of Nigerian jurisprudence in that it asserts the real recognition of a community that exists under the law.

The promulgation of the bill is linked to a particularly brutal event: the execution of Saro-Wiwa and nine other Ogoni activists. After rioting in May 1994 during which four Ogoni leaders were murdered, Ken Saro-Wiwa and his nine co-accused found themselves before a Civil Disturbances Special Tribunal. Later, an ad hoc tribunal was established for their trial. Reviewing the case, the special rapporteur for the UN found that the rioting had resulted from government agents stirring up dissent between the Ogoni and neighboring ethnic groups. The tribunal itself was constituted in contravention of due process. Following procedures established by the military government, the judges (including an army officer) were appointed by the executive.[63] As the United Nations report points out, this was in direct contravention of the basic principle of the right to trial by an impartial court. The constitution of a tribunal in such a way is also in breach of the African Charter of Human and Peoples' Rights (article 7, article 26) and the International Covenant on Civil and Political Rights (article 14.1). Indeed, a challenge was filed in the constitutional court but not heard. There were further serious breaches of due process in the conduct of the trial, including exclusion of evidence that shed serious doubt on the prosecution's case. This was accompanied by military harassment of defense counsel.

The tribunal pronounced the death penalty. In the face of this abuse of due process, what possible recourse was there? There is a record of the speech made by Saro-Wiwa before the court that ordered his execution. We must consider some fragments. First,

> We all stand before history. I am a man of peace, of ideas.[64]

Saro-Wiwa inverts the scene of his trial. Although he has just been found guilty, although he has just been condemned, he affirms the existence of a wider jurisdiction, a force of justice that will judge those who have judged him. The trope serves to generalize the idea of the trial:

> We all stand before history. I and my colleagues are not the only ones on trial. Shell is here on trial.[65]

If history has the force of judgment, then the trial is most properly that of the company that needs to be held accountable for its crimes against a people. It is not simply a company that needs to be held responsible but a political order, a conjunction of multinational business and the nation state:

> On trial also is the Nigerian nation, its present rulers and those who assist them. Any nation which can do to the weak and disadvantaged what the Nigerian nation has done to the Ogoni, loses a claim to independence and to freedom from outside influence.[66]

This is a bold claim. We will, presently, investigate the precise constitution of this argument, for Saro-Wiwa is making explicit reference to a jurisprudential theme, to a justice that would privilege human rights over the sovereignty of the state. At this point, the whole history of Nigerian independence is suspended. In this moment, colonial and postcolonial legal and political orders are conflated; a different jurisdiction is imagined. The genius of this claim goes even further. Saro-Wiwa makes reference to the "riddle of the Niger delta." In one sense, this is a glyph for the struggle of the oppressed for their rights; in another sense, it is a universal scene that is evoked as divine justice:

> For the Holy Quran says in Sura 42, verse 41: "All those that fight when oppressed incur no guilt, but Allah shall punish the oppressor." Come the day.[67]

This is a sublime theme invoking a justice that goes beyond any specific juristic manifestation. It is at this level that Saro-Wiwa can articulate a frame that is sufficient to his theme, a justice that addresses itself to peoples and their exploitation. But it is not just this utopian jurisdiction; this law to come. Saro-Wiwa is making a claim in the present. Just as the bill of rights, of which he was an author, makes the Ogoni case into a general one, his own struggle becomes a universal struggle for "a fair and just democratic system that protects everyone and every ethnic group and gives us all a valid claim to human civilisation." Just as his struggle is a universal struggle, it is inseparable from the triumph of the human soul: neither "imprisonment nor death can stop our ultimate victory."

Continuing Injustices against the Ogoni

Let us reconsider one of the central claims of this speech. For Saro-Wiwa, the Nigerian state has lost any claim to its legitimacy through its treatment of the Ogoni: it "loses a claim to independence and to freedom from outside influence." What could this mean? One clear sense of this statement is the invoking of a universal or global notion of human rights. A state must be held illegitimate to the extent that it violates the human rights of its citizens. Those who petitioned Saro-Wiwa's case before the African Commission took up this challenge. The commission affirmed that numerous breaches of the charter had taken place. What we need to do, though, is to examine the extent to which both this decision and a later one suggest the outlines of a jurisprudence that could reinvent and invigorate a notion of democracy. How can the Nigerian state's duties to its citizens be framed?

The decision of 1999 affirmed that there had been a breach of article 5 of the African charter. Saro-Wiwa and his codefendants had been subject to ill treatment during their imprisonment and interrogation. The government had effectively failed to recognize the "legal status" of the human being. Breaches of article 4, which protects the inviolability of the human being, support this argument. There were also breaches of articles 6 and 7. These articles can be read as a protection of due process, specifically aimed at outlawing arbitrary detention and at specifying the standards that must govern the way in which a trial is conducted. The federal government had also failed to uphold its obligations under article 10, which affirms the right of free association. If this decision can be seen as focused, essentially, on the conduct of the trial, the later decision can be read as a broader consideration of the government's treatment of the Ogoni.

In the decision of 2001, the commission determined that the Nigerian government was in breach of a number of articles of the charter.[68] Note how this decision is concerned with the economic rights and duties of the state. Although the federal government is entitled to produce oil, this entitlement is qualified by certain duties and obligations. Article 21 is precise in stressing that exploitation of natural resources is to be undertaken in an equitable manner and in the interests of "the people." Where degradation has occurred as a result of industrial extraction of natural resources, those peoples affected have the right to compensation. Furthermore, the article specifies that the African government should work to "eliminate all forms of foreign economic exploitation" by multinational corporations and "international monopolies." The cases to which the commission refers stress that governments have a duty to protect their citizens against acts by private parties,[69] a proposition supported by cases under other human rights instruments.[70]

The commission also argued that the Nigerian government had violated two further articles of the charter. Article 24 places on the state the duty to preserve the environment to the extent that it is "favourable" to people's "development." Article 16 relates to manifold duties on the state to safeguard the mental and physical health of individuals. The government had breached both articles, as it had participated in the pollution of the environment, caused harm to the peoples of the Delta region, and had failed to protect both the people and the environment from the degradation caused by the Shell consortium. The Nigerian government was also in breach of the obligation to undertake studies of the Ogoni lands with a view toward assessing damage to the region. Those arguments were run alongside a claim that the government had not guaranteed the right to property under article 14 and, drawing on a number of articles, that the right to shelter had also been infringed by the destruction of Ogoni villages. The commission also accepted arguments on the infringement of the right to food. Although this was not directly stated in the charter, it was a clear implication of reading together the articles protecting the right to life (article 1); the right to health (article 16); and the right to economic, social, and cultural development (article 22).

Although this case has been criticized,[71] there is a sense in which it represents an important intervention in the political development of African democracy. To return to our main point, it would seem that the promise of democracy to protect the local, to create the nation that can preserve the sovereignty of peoples, comes about through a general or global discourse on human rights. However, within the general application of human rights principles, the nation retains its importance. This takes us to a nexus of concerns. There is a negative aspect to this positing of the nation. During the period of military rule, the provisions in the Nigerian Constitution that incorporated the African Charter on Human and Peoples' Rights had been suspended by the military. The fact that there was now a civilian administration suggests that there would also be a return to due process and a renewed commitment to human rights. The commission noted, however, that the Nigerian government had not responded to communications about the availability of domestic remedies, and hence the status of the charter in Nigerian law was uncertain. Moreover, the Nigerian government acknowledged that there were ongoing abuses of the Ogoni and their land by oil companies operating in the region.

So, the criticisms that have rightly fastened on the ultimate weakness of the charter at the level of the remedies that it is able to invoke are, in part, drawing attention to the failure of this discourse at perhaps its most vital level. The commission's decision merely reminds the Nigerian government of the matter's importance. Although there is a symbolic importance to this type of utterance, it leaves a great deal to be desired in terms of compensation for the abuses suffered. In response to the commission, the Nigerian government acknowledged the seriousness of the Ogoni issue and outlined the response of the administration. They had set up a properly resourced Federal Ministry of Environment with a brief that focused on the Ogoni region and the Niger delta; a Judicial Commission of Inquiry has been instituted to examine the alleged human rights abuses, and Ogoni petitions have been considered. Whether this is sufficient must remain, at this stage, an open question. However, an issue clearly raised by the Ogoni case is the responsibility of international business, the extent to which corporations can be seen as liable for human rights abuses.

What wider conclusions can we draw about these decisions? The discourse of the charter works by according the state its proper rights and privileges but also by seeing them as qualified by the obligations that the state has toward its peoples. We can see, though, that the charter also attempts to create a viable human rights regime by making the state responsible for the actions of those industries that are working within the state's territory. Taken together, the decisions can be seen as the law's recommendation of certain minimum political forms. Consider the rights to due process, fair trial, and the minimum commitments to social and economic rights. Might these represent the *Grundnorm*, the founding principle of the Nigerian Independence Constitution? The fact that they meet with the consent of the majority also gets around the problem regarding the coercive nature of the fundamental norm that had been such a concern in Nigerian legal philosophy. Might there also be found here a conjunction between law and economy? A legal prescription for a form of economic relationships that have to protect and sustain life?

Justice and Rights

What do the Ogoni case and the intervention of the commission mean for a way of thinking about Nigerian jurisprudence? Can we see this as a response to the global? Taking together Saro-Wiwa's words and the aspirations of the charter, we could affirm the priority of justice to law. We might be able to say that justice is the mode of law's appearance: "it is justice that enables law to appear in any society as an acceptable norm";[72] or, to gloss this statement, it is a question of a law that serves the people. One commentator suggests that justice can be understood as "protection from power," a formula that acknowledges that law is the product of powerful interest groups who control the state and that the role of the courts is to protect citizens from "wrong and arbitrary power."[73] If there is a human rights discourse, if there is a response to abuses of human rights on a continental scale, could this be its touchstone? A state is only legitimate to the extent that it can protect the sovereignty of its people. We have then perhaps been concerned with a struggle between different discourses of rights. The execution of Saro-Wiwa represents a fracture, perhaps even a turning point, where the promises made at independence, the promises taken up in Nigerian jurisprudence, the promise for a democracy worthy of its name are seen in a stark light. Can there be an African jurisprudence that founds the law on justice?

Notes

1. On the riddle of the nation, see Peter Fitzpatrick, *Modernism and the Grounds of Law* (Cambridge: Cambridge University Press, 2001). On the conjunction of nation and law, see Peter Goodrich, *Languages of Law* (London: Weidenfield and Nicholson, 1990).

2. Obafemi Awolowo, *Path to Nigerian Freedom* (London: Faber, 1957), 58. On the writing of nation, see Homi Bhaba, *The Location of Culture* (New York: Routledge, 1994). See also, Achille Mbembe, *On the Postcolony* (Berkeley: University of California Press, 2001).

3. Awolowo, *Path to Nigerian Freedom*, 20.

4. Egosha Osaghae, *Crippled Giant: Nigeria since Independence* (London: Hurst, 1998), 36.

5. Osaghae, *Crippled Giant*, 90. See also, Oluwole Idowu Odumosu, *The Nigerian Constitution: History and Development* (Lagos, Nigeria: African University Press, 1963), esp. 226–75, on the tensions between federalism and localism.

6. Osaghae, *Crippled Giant*, 91.

7. Osaghae, *Crippled Giant*, 89.

8. Ken Saro-Wiwa, *Genocide in Nigeria: The Ogoni Tragedy* (Lagos, Nigeria: Saros International, 1992), 20.

9. Saro-Wiwa, *Genocide in Nigeria*, 20.

10. The political problems inherited by the independent state have their roots in the colonial order. Colonialism fostered strong central institutions

rather than participatory democracy. Nigerian scholars have dubbed the period up to 1946 as that of "complete subordination." Governmental power over Nigeria rested in the hands of the governor; the country had been split into two protectorates, one in the north and one in the south, and over this vast territory, the governor was both "sole executive and legislature." B. O. Nwabueze, *A Constitutional History of Nigeria* (London: Hurst, 1983), 36. For a broader account of the structure of colonial law and government, see Mahmood Mamdani, *Citizen and Subject: Contemporary Africa and the Legacy of Late Colonialism* (London: James Currey, 1996).

11. Nwabueze, *Constitutional History*, 26.

12. J. A. Gana, "The Impact of External Economic Forces on Nigeria's Political Economy," in *The Nigerian Economy: A Political Economy Approach*, ed. the Nigerian Economic Society (Lagos, Nigeria: Longman, 1986), 126–42, 144.

13. Gana, "Impact of External Economic Forces," 47.

14. Osaghae, *Crippled Giant*, 50.

15. Osaghae, *Crippled Giant*, 48.

16. Osaghae, *Crippled Giant*, 47.

17. Human Rights Watch, *The Price of Oil: Corporate Responsibility and Human Rights Violations in Nigeria's Oil Producing Communities* (New York: Human Rights Watch, 1999), 27.

18. Human Rights Watch, *Price of Oil*, 27.

19. Human Rights Watch, *Price of Oil*, 21.

20. Human Rights Watch, *Price of Oil*, 21.

21. Osaghae, *Crippled Giant*, 68–77.

22. Osaghae, *Crippled Giant*, 79–90.

23. Osaghae, *Crippled Giant*, 97.

24. Osaghae, *Crippled Giant*, 97.

25. Osaghae, *Crippled Giant*, 104.

26. Osaghae, *Crippled Giant*, 155–56.

27. Osaghae, *Crippled Giant*, 170.

28. William D. Graf, *The Nigerian State: Political Economy, State Class, and Political System in the Post-Colonial Era to 1988* (London: Heinemann, 1988).

29. Adebayo Olukoshi, "The Politics of Structural Adjustment," in *Crisis and Adjustment in the Nigerian Economy* (Lagos: JAD Publishers, 1991), 159–79, at 161.

30. Richard Synge, *Nigeria: The Way Forward* (London: Euromoney Books, 1993).

31. Synge, *Nigeria*, 197.

32. Olukoshi, *Crisis and Adjustment*, 161.

33. Osaghae, *Crippled Giant*, 204.

34. Osaghae, *Crippled Giant*, 281.

35. Osaghae, *Crippled Giant*, 281.

36. Osaghae, *Crippled Giant*, 282.

37. Kayode Eso, *Thoughts on Law and Jurisprudence* (Lagos, Nigeria: MIJ Professional Publishers, 1990), 80.

38. Eso, *Thoughts on Law*, 80.

39. Eso, *Thoughts on Law*, 34.

40. Eso, *Thoughts on Law*, 38.

41. Eso, *Thoughts on Law*, 41.

42. *Akintola v. Adegbenro*, 1962 1 All NLR 431.

43. *Lakanmi v. AG*, 1971 1 UILR 201.

44. At least in the sense that one might find in Austin or Salmond.

45. Taslim Olawale Elias, *Groundwork of Nigerian Law* (London: Routledge/ K. Paul, 1954), 16. See also, T. O. Elias, *Towards a Common Law in Nigeria* (Lagos, Nigeria: University of Lagos, 1972), 254–73; and Elias, *Nigerian Essays in Jurisprudence*, ed. T. O. Elias and M. I. Jegede (Lagos, Nigeria: MIJ Publishers, 1993).

46. Eso, *Thoughts on Law*, 258. See also, B. O. Nwabueze, *Military Rule and Constitutionalism* (Ibadan, Nigeria: Spectrum, 1992). Nwabueze argues that the resolution of Nigeria's "socio-economic problems" demands "a system which can aggregate and reconcile competing societal demands" (325). This is not provided by military dictatorship. See also, Epiphany Azinge, *Law Making under Military Regimes* (Benin City, Nigeria: Oliz, 1994).

47. Eso, *Thoughts on Law*, 261.

48. *Olawoyin v. Commissioner of Police*, 1961 1 All NLR 203.

49. Eso, *Thoughts on Law*, 275.

50. Eso, *Thoughts on Law*, 18.

51. Saro-Wiwa, *Genocide in Nigeria*, 89.

52. Saro-Wiwa, *Genocide in Nigeria*, 25.

53. Saro-Wiwa, *Genocide in Nigeria*, 12.

54. Saro-Wiwa, *Genocide in Nigeria*, 15.

55. Saro-Wiwa, *Genocide in Nigeria*, 17.

56. Saro-Wiwa, *Genocide in Nigeria*, 43.

57. Saro-Wiwa, *Genocide in Nigeria*, 63.

58. Human Rights Watch, *The Price of Oil*.

59. Human Rights Watch, *The Price of Oil*, 75–76.

60. Human Rights Watch, *The Price of Oil*, 77.

61. Saro-Wiwa, *Genocide in Nigeria*, 78–79.

62. Saro-Wiwa, *Genocide in Nigeria*, 78–79.

63. The tribunal itself was probably acting *ultra vires* under its own enabling statute, as there had been no prior setting up of a civil disturbance committee.

64. At http://archive.greenpeace.org/comms/ken/state.html.

65. At http://archive.greenpeace.org/comms/ken/state.html.

66. At http://archive.greenpeace.org/comms/ken/state.html.

67. At http://archive.greenpeace.org/comms/ken/state.html.

68. African Commission on Human and Peoples' Rights, *Decisions on Communications before the African Commission*, 155/96 at www.achpt.org/html/communications.html. See also, UN General Assembly, Fifty-first Session, Agenda item 110(c), *Human Rights Questions: Human Rights Situations and Reports of Special Rapporteurs and Representatives*, at www.un.org/documents/ga/docs/51/plenary/a51–538.htm. On the African charter, see Malcolm Evans and Rachel Murray, eds., *The African Charter of Human and Peoples' Rights* (Cambridge: Cambridge University Press, 2002).

69. Union des Jeunes Avocats/Chad, Communication 74/94.

70. *Velasquez Rodriguez v. Honduras*, Inter-American Court of Human Rights, Judgment of July 19, 1988, Series C, No. 4; and also *X and Y v. Netherlands*, 91 ECHR (1985) (Ser. A) at 32.

71. Gina Bekker, Caste Note, *Journal of African Law*, volume 47, issue 01. April 2003: 126–32.

72. Eso, *Thoughts on Law*, 253.

73. C. A. Oputa, *The Judiciary under the Military Regime* (Lagos, Nigeria: University of Lagos, 1997), 77.

THE HONOR OF A PAUPER'S OATH: THE INSTITUTIONS OF THE INTERNATIONAL ECONOMIC LEGAL ORDER

> This heavy, implacable cloud, burning and alive with the insane, the indissoluble will of the fetish by which we are compelled to live.
>
> —Henri Lefebvre, *Notes for a Critique of Everyday Life*

International economic law presents a challenge to legal theory.[1] In the introduction, we looked at the distinctions between hard and soft law and argued that international economic law uses both these legal forms to create a regime for international regulation.[2] In this chapter, we will see that essential elements of this regime are those exceptions or special policies that determine the legal status of developing nations in the world trade and financial systems. Key notions such as conditionality will be seen as the conjunction of legal and economic measures in the creation of governance regimes for debtor nations.[3] We will also need to examine the constitutional structure of GATT/WTO and study the notion of the exception.

Some may object that by looking at international economic law from the perspective of the developing world, we are bound to create a skewed reading.[4] However, for reasons that I hope will be plain from the first chapter, we can defend this approach by suggesting that world economy is based on fundamental inequalities. To develop this thesis in any convincing sense is impossible within this short book. Our focus must therefore be on the structure of a legal regime that has not yet resolved, and may be unable to resolve, the structuring economic inequalities that it seeks to regulate.

One further caveat is necessary. This chapter does not seek to argue that the soft law and hard law regimes can be strictly demarcated and opposed. There are a number of elements to this argument. First, the soft law–hard law distinction cannot easily be correlated with an argument that either regime is necessarily a better way of structuring relations between developing nations and international institutions. In other words, one cannot afford to approach this area with any simplistic idea that soft law favors the developed world and that hard law favors the undeveloped world. We also need to understand that with the construction of a coherent dispute-handling mechanism, the WTO has become the most "legal" of the institutions that we are considering; but this again is not necessarily an unqualified good for developing nations. The economic location of developing nations within world trade and finance means that analysis must always begin at the level of structural complexity rather than take a legal problematic as definitive.

"And in His Waste House, Detritus": The IMF and the World Bank

The legal structuring of the IMF is achieved through an interplay of hard and soft law, a conjunction of policy and principle.[5] Let us engage with this concern by considering the IMF's Articles of Association. As the IMF is autointerpreting, its constitutional structure is dissimilar to those orders that characterize democracies. Interpretative and executive functions are blurred in IMF policy decisions. However, this needs to be set against the fact that some of the IMF's foundational articles do create more formally "binding" obligations for its members. Distinguishing between the hard and soft aspects of the IMF's articles takes us to political considerations, or, to be precise, those resistances where nations have affirmed their sovereignty against the power of the IMF. When we turn to study conditionality, we will see that soft law largely structures the doctrine. This avoids the limitations on freedom of maneuver that strict legal obligations would create.

Let us approach this issue through the IMF's own understanding of its purposes, as outlined in the first article. The IMF is described as a permanent coordinating body that encourages "monetary cooperation" (1.1). Through the coordination and consultation functions of the IMF, a "balanced growth of international trade" achieves "high levels of employment," "real income," and the development of national economies. Article 1.3 specifies the centrality of "exchange stability" and "orderly exchange arrangements" as key aspects of this balanced international order. The intersection of currency and trade concerns can be appreciated in article 1.4, which details the IMF's role in assuring that a "multilateral system of payments" for "current transactions" are put in place and that trade restrictions are relaxed. Another central task of the fund is to offer "temporary" financial help with "adequate safeguards" to member nations having difficulties with balance of payments. The safeguards must ensure that the overriding objectives of international stability are achieved. Article 1.4 returns to the concern with balance of payments, specifying a maintenance of equilibrium at an international level.

The IMF's policy on exchange rates creates the terms that apply to any nation wanting to enter the world's economic community. Put crudely, IMF policy attempts to ensure stable currency exchange and prevent destabilizing international speculation.[6] These are the prime means through which the IMF can ensure currency stability and hence maintain the functioning of international markets. However, it is important to bear in mind the warning that article 1 is broad in scope and cannot be seen as laying down specific legal duties, unless later articles make these duties precise.[7] Perhaps the reason is that governments are reluctant to allow intervention in the area of currency control, a matter over which a nation should have sovereignty. At the same time, the IMF considers a member nation as being under a "legal obligation" to carry out its commitments once the nation becomes a member.[8] What does this mean? How can we understand this mixture of duty and discretion? We need to examine some of the most important articles.

Article 4.4.a concerns the stability of exchange rates. The article places a tripartite duty on a member state: to achieve stable exchange rates, to maintain orderly exchange arrangements with other nations, and to desist from alteration of exchange rates. The consensus of legal understanding holds that this article does not impose a workable legal regime. Originally, currencies were pegged against the U.S. dollar, which was fixed to the gold standard. In 1971 this system failed when the United States pulled out of the agreement.[9] The new article, introduced in 1978, effectively places the management of exchange rates within the discretion of individual nations through a variety of mechanisms. For Mann, this suggests that there is no "realistic legal duty to ensure the international stability of currencies."[10] Other commentators see the new article 4 as a part of a series of "soft" recommendations that refer to underlying economic objectives.[11] This is not surprising if one considers that the operation of an exchange rate is only one factor that can result in the stability of exchanges.[12] This article, then, appears to offer an international code of practice, a "code of conduct" for economic good governance.[13] The only example of breach, the Swedish devaluation of the krona in October 1982, did not result in the imposition of a sanction.[14] The lack of punishment suggests that the article is not an example of a hard law provision.

For a thorough understanding of the IMF regime, it would be necessary to see article 4 in the context of the other controls placed over the international movements of money. As space is restricted in this book, we cannot analyze in detail the cluster of articles that regulate current and capital transactions, but we can make a couple of general points. First, it is difficult to maintain a hard and fast distinction between capital transactions and current transactions, although the effect of the relevant articles is to determine two distinct regimes for their governance.[15] In relation to current transactions, articles 8 and 14.2 contain, even in their amended forms, the central notion of currency conversion, or the free exchange of one currency for another.[16] Article 8 states a definite legal obligation;[17] indeed, "truly fundamental rights and duties" are laid down. The article refers to payments for international transactions.[18] Lying behind this article and the regime it envisages is the issue of convertibility that is fundamental to the buying and selling of currency in international trade. Government intervention is only acceptable within certain narrowly defined limits (8.2).[19] This can be joined to a nation's nonparticipation in "discriminatory" currency practices (article 8.3), which result in distortions of trade as payments are restricted or prevented. Although there appears to be no "exchange control" over movements of capital,[20] commentators suggest that IMF policy favors a liberal regime for the "orderly and sustainable" management of financial flows.[21] The need for control on capital transactions reflects fears that, without restrictions, capital movements would take place with little regard for the sovereignty of national governments. The overall effect of the article is the establishing of "market mechanisms" for currency transactions.[22]

These articles thus suggest that the international movement of money and the maintenance of stable and convertible currencies can be regulated through the coordination of those fundamental duties that are in the hands of sovereign governments and the overseeing powers of an international agency. We need to see this aspect of the IMF's work alongside the provision of financial assistance to developing nations. It is as if one face of the IMF is turned toward the maintenance of the existing system while the other face is turned toward those nations who remain outside the circle of the privileged. We could also ask questions about the nature of obligations that developing nations assume in their dealings with the IMF. Are these obligations merely discretionary, or are they binding? The most intriguing issues around the nature of IMF obligations are concerned with the notion of conditionality. We need to look at the structure of conditionality in an attempt to clarify this issue. Although conditionality is based on the articles of the IMF, it is also structured by a combination of hard law, discretion, and soft law mechanisms.

The IMF functions as a fund that can be drawn on to help nations in difficulties with balance of payments.[23] The drawing rights that member states have over the communal fund are contentious. Originally, there was a quota system that linked borrowing rights to contributions determined by a nation's position in the world economy.[24] However, there were concerns over the nature of these borrowing rights. The needs of debtor nations were different from those of nations expecting to be creditors.[25] Nations in the former group favored automatic borrowing rights, while those in the latter category preferred stricter controls that would make borrowing dependent on undertakings by debtors to meet certain requirements. In was in this context that articles 5.3 and 5.5 were interpreted as giving rise to the doctrine of conditionality (although as we will see, other articles are also important for the doctrine's development).[26]

Conditionality is complex, and we can only consider it in crudest outline. It can be understood as the doctrine that relates to the commitments that a national government must make when it draws from the fund. For example, conditions may be attached to control public expenditure, control inflation, or promote the liberalization of trade.[27] The difficulties of characterizing the operation of the IMF can be seen in the debate over the precise nature of conditionality.[28] In what ways does hard law determine the doctrine? Questions have also been asked about the nature of a "drawing." Is it a loan or an international agreement?[29] One conclusion that could be drawn from these debates is that the arrangements were left deliberately ambiguous. This would allow the IMF to respond differently to different situations rather than be limited by any settled doctrine.

Leaving these issues aside, we can suggest that conditionality has been elaborated in such a way as to create significant differences in the way in which the IMF treats developed and developing nations. To appreciate this point, we need to look at the construction of conditionality, which takes us back to the Articles of Association. To qualify for a drawing, the member nation must show that its economic circumstances are such that the action is necessary (article 5). Article 4.3 describes the terms that apply. The first is drawn quite broadly: the purpose for which the drawing is made must be coherent with "the Fund's policies." Article 4.1 states that member nations are obligated to cooperate with the IMF, and this stipulation has led to the practice of periodic consultations over the "stability of exchange rates."[30] Article 5.3 empowers the IMF to place "adequate safeguards" on use of drawings from the fund. One commentator has argued that "the virtual absence of compulsion in Article IV consultation stands in sharp contrast to the mandatory surveillance in balance of payments support."[31] The practice of the IMF has been such that developing nations with balance-of-payments deficits have been subjected to the "hard law" regime of "adequate safeguards" while developed nations have been subject to no more than the soft law regime of article IV consultations.[32] One can appreciate how the IMF's practice has made for an inequitable development of the legal regime relating to conditionality.

A distinction can be made between the formal structure of conditionality that relates back to the Articles of Association and the associated "guidelines" drawn up by the Executive Board. Guidelines cover the precise standards or benchmarks to be applied to the assessment of a nation's compliance with the terms of the loan, the degree of penetration into the economy of the borrower, and the extent to which the IMF can set targets. Guidelines that relate directly to the articles state binding obligations, but not all sets of guidelines operate in this way.[33] Indeed, nonobligatory guidelines are a good example of soft law. From a legal perspective, then, we are quite far from a notion of a regime that creates universal binding obligations and closer to a discretionary regime where rules or principles are interpreted flexibly. The issue, then, is how the discretion of the fund is structured. We will see that it is essentially a pragmatic response to political events, rather than the application of a legal logic.

In other words, to understand the development of conditionality, we have to place it in the context of the IMF's policies. One can observe a gradual shift in the operation and implementation of conditionality. At the end of the 1970s, developed Western nations made use of IMF loans. This can be contrasted to the present situation, where mainly developing nations make use of the facility.[34] In 1978–1979, the Guidelines on Conditionality were issued as a response to criticisms of the fund's activities. They describe a managed process whereby money is made available to the extent that performance criteria are satisfied. These criteria tend to concern macroeconomic issues and can vary according to the problems that led to the drawings in the first place. Although allowances can be made for the specific circumstances of any given country, services can be suspended if a client nation continues to show an inability to control its economy satisfactorily. But to what extent can the specific problems of developing nations be taken into account? The IMF has argued that there should be no "discrimination" in the application of economic conditions. As Southern nations suffer from their subordinate location in world economy, the fund should discriminate in its dealings with them. Formal equality cannot be a justification for applying standards that might be suitable to developed Western economies but are detrimental to the struggling economies of poorer nations.

The fund responded to the problems of the developing world by making available certain special facilities. Lowenfeld argues that in recent years article 5 has served as a way of structuring the IMF's response in these instances.[35] For example, the "compensatory financing facility" was designed to assist developing nations dependent on the export of a single or restricted set of commodities.[36] The extended fund facility made for a longer period over which larger drawings from the IMF could be made. However, as the debt crisis became more intense in the middle of the 1990s, a new approach was required. Working alongside the World Bank, the Heavily Indebted Poor Country (HIPC) initiative was developed and tailored to meet the needs of countries that had exhausted whatever special measures might be available. The complete relief of Third World debt was seen as imprudent, an act of charity that would not encourage sustainable development or economic control. Indeed, there was a continuing need to monitor a nation's performance and ensure structural reforms. A second major input of the fund in the alleviation of debt is the Poverty Reduction and Growth Facility.[37] This fund is composed of donations, borrowings, and sales of the fund's own holdings in gold. Although there are conditions that apply to the award of the facility, they are considered to be more relaxed than those of the HIPC initiative, and at present there are a number of countries "benefiting" from the loans at the preferential rates that the fund can offer. The political dynamics of this fund can be glimpsed, however, if one considers the loan made to Pakistan in 2001 as a "return"[38] for the assistance that that country offered in the war against terror.[39]

The International Bank for Reconstruction and Development

The IMF has to be seen as operating alongside the International Bank for Reconstruction and Development (hereafter, the World Bank). Indeed, the problems that the IMF experienced in offering funds for nations with balance-of-payment difficulties meant that the functions of the World Bank and the IMF became somewhat blurred.[40] Our focus will be on the bank's powers to lend and structure loans, and we will return to the key problematic as developed in the previous section. Like the IMF, the bank's lending policy reflects a series of ad hoc policy decisions rather than evidence of a coherent development of specifically legal principles. Objectives are developed through projects and programs. Projects concern investments in the development of civil infrastructure, whereas programs are more broadly defined development interventions.[41]

We will be concerned first of all with the World Bank's input to the doctrine of conditionality.[42] How can this term be defined from the bank's perspective? We need to begin with an understanding of the investment vehicles that may be made available to a nation. Depending on the outcome of an overall review regarding a nation's economic condition and the development problems that it faces, the bank can arrange investment loans and adjustment loans. Whereas the former can cover a range of sectors, including "financing goods, works and services," the latter provide "quick-disbursing external financing" to enable reform. Thus, conditionality can be understood as a control device that links financial measures to the implementation of the broader reform program. As the bank puts it, "Commitment to reform is essential, and conditionality can usefully reinforce . . . the success of reforms supported under adjustment loans." The terms can of course be adapted in relation to a particular nation and its needs, both before the loan is made and once the funds become available. We can therefore suggest that conditionality is the way in which a reform program is monitored and policed by the bank itself.[43]

In other words, this area of the regulation of money is characterized by "soft law." Article 4.4.c lays down the conditions that are attached to the modification of loans. The threshold for relief is "acute exchange contingency," which suggests that the problem of debt relates to a nation's location within a network of world trade and the movement of money. Exchange stringency means that the debtor is unable to service the loans in the required currency. In this situation, the debtor may apply to the bank for a "relaxation" in the terms of the repayment. Criteria for the bank's agreement to such a relaxation are framed in wide terms. There needs to be satisfaction that the conditions are in the interests of the debtor, the "operations of the Bank," and the "members as a whole." Recourse can then be made to one of two options that are again framed in terms of the bank's discretion and not as a binding legal duty. The first option is to allow payments in the members' own currency for a period of up to three years (once certain conditions have been put into place in relation to the exchange rate of the currency) and for the repurchase of the currency at a later date. The second option is to "modify" the terms for the repayment of the debt or extend the terms of the loan. This section works alongside article 7.a, which applies in case of default. Again, the section is framed in discretionary terms: the bank may "make such arrangements as may be feasible" to amend the obligations under the loan agreement.

Just as the IMF's guidelines are essentially policy tools, the World Bank's articles must be interpreted in terms of the actual practice, although it is not clear whether any particular decisions are considered binding or persuasive precedents. The first prospectus, issued in the early years of the bank's operations, alludes to the discretion to modify the terms of loans. However, after the modification of the loans to Paraguay, India, and Haiti in the 1950s, the prospectus did no more than refer to the board's discretion under the bank's articles to make decisions in light of economic conditions. Likewise, the decision in 1968 to reschedule the loans that had been made to India was justified by reference to "macro-economics."[44] After a period of actively restructuring loans in the 1960s, the bank seemed to change policy and stated that it no longer engaged in this practice—a position that was repeated until the end of the 1980s and probably reflects the economic turbulence of those times, in particular the problems with the price of oil. Despite the public statement to the contrary, the World Bank's response to political situations was seen as its modifying (or rescheduling) certain loans.[45]

After the independence of Bangladesh from Pakistan in 1975, the terms of certain loans had to be reworked to reflect the emergence of this new sovereign nation. The package was justified by reference to economic considerations.[46] Political events also lay behind the reworking of loans to Nicaragua in 1975. Despite later initiatives in Latin America and Europe, the practice was never officially articulated until 1991, when the bank stated a "rights accumulation policy."[47] The policy was motivated by the need to assist debtor nations with the service of their loans and was based on the notion of their achieving and sustaining economic stability. As part of this process, the bank acted as a nation's sponsor, obtaining funding from other sources. The cost of assistance was the bank's assumed right to direct the economic affairs of the debtor nation and to stipulate objectives that would allow the satisfaction of both the bank's debt and that of other creditors. This practice became the bank's official position. Debtors were to be assisted, but the bank was to assume control over important aspects of their economy and initiate reforms aimed at "structural adjustment and stabilization."[48]

What conclusions can be drawn from this practice? There is, first of all, a distinction between those countries that default "willfully" and those that are unable to repay for reasons they cannot control.[49] The former situation allows a certain flexibility to reschedule the loan; in the latter case, the bank is empowered by its articles to take whatever steps are possible. Lying behind this distinction is the need to prevent the bank from having to call for funds from other member nations so that it can honor its own obligations. Thus, the notion based on the language of article 4.4.c—that a debtor nation has a "right" to petition the bank for different terms, with an obligation on the bank to accept those terms—may not be accurate. It is economics, rather than law, that determines policy. Likewise, the flexibility given under the articles, and the repeated practice of not referring to the articles to justify decisions, suggests that the role played by hard or soft law is minimal. As Lowenfeld suggests, this policy has been followed because the bank itself "relies on the market for the funding of its operations."[50] The bank prefers a "cooperative" approach to ensure the smooth operation of the international community of financiers.

GATT Jurisprudence

In comparison with the work of the IMF and the World Bank, the work of GATT and the WTO may appear far more "legal." What difference does this formality make to the governance regime that relates to developing nations? Answering this question demands that we look at the broader foundational ideas of trade regulation that underlie GATT. We will see that despite its distinctive legal beginnings that stressed universal rules, GATT soon mutated. Attempting to hold together a coherent structure of universal norms and the special requirements of developing nations, GATT set forth a particular notion of the exception that accommodated developing nations into a regime regulating world trade.

The origins of GATT lie in the Proposals for Expansion of World Trade and Employment, circulated by the United States between 1946 and 1948, and the General Agreement signed in Geneva in 1947.[51] Distinguishing GATT from the other international bodies created at Bretton Woods was a legalistic input. As commentators have stressed, GATT rules were meant to be "contractual."[52] GATT attempted to give broad principles a precise formulation as binding rules and envisaged a jurisdiction that extended beyond the merely internal procedural concerns of its own constitutional composition.

However, as GATT developed, the legalism of its conception was compromised. In the wider literature, this tends to be associated with a

69

distinction between rigidity and flexibility, or legalism and pragmatism.[53] For a start, there was no clear sense of the sanctions that would be used to punish miscreants or deter breaches of the rules.[54] Over time, it also appeared that the broader modus operandi of GATT was less than legalistic. "Discrepancies" in terms of the obligations or duties of the contracting parties met with two responses. One approach was to "change the rule of GATT so as to legitimise the divergent practice"; a second course of action was merely to ignore the breach of the rules and hope that "one day return would be made to the rule" or that maybe the breach would constitute a new rule.[55] "Adaptability" became a mark of the system's legitimacy, a measure of its capacity to develop in light of events. A study of GATT jurisprudence, then, must be prepared to balance principles against the mechanisms that exist for modifying, qualifying, or changing those principles.

What also marks GATT (and WTO jurisprudence) is the manner in which these bodies have taken on a dispute resolution function. This important theme is considered first in an overview and then is developed in the following section as part of the broader consideration of world trade. The need to move from consensus and conciliation to formal legalism was, for some, a kind of fall from grace. Although adjudication was originally based on articles 22 and 23, it developed through the customary procedures of member nations. Trade disputes were resolved through negotiation, becoming slightly more formal as time developed through the constitution of panels by the GATT secretariat. Thus, "GATT success in the 1950s could be traced to its membership, which consisted of a group of like minded nations and diplomats."[56] GATT's cohesion was ruined by the influx of developing nations. Represented by the Group of 77, the consensus approach clearly did not suit the group members' interests. Under further pressure caused by the formation of the EU, the old approach to dispute resolution broke down.

The Tokyo round of negotiations (addressed later in this chapter) saw further moves toward a more legalistic method of adjudication. There was a belief among developed nations that a more coherent legal regime was required to protect them from the more powerful contracting members.[57] At the same time, though, the United States was active in bringing cases against developing nations and against European nations that had preferential trade arrangements with former colonial territories. In terms of the early development of the case law in this area,

70

the reliance on defenses available under part IV of GATT acted as a restraint on litigation against less-developed contracting members.[58] The mode of dispute resolution, however, privileged the "mediating" approach rather than the "judgmental."[59] In the early eighties, however, a strange alliance developed between the United States and developing nations, with both blocs believing that advantages could be gained by moving toward a reshaped adjudication process. The Uruguay round of negotiations was to see far reaching reforms.

As explained later in the chapter, the Uruguay round also saw the foundation of the WTO. In relation to the dispute resolution procedures, though, the years immediately after the birth of the WTO produced more litigation against developing countries. Under GATT developing nations preferred to opt out of the negotiations rather than pursue formal procedures.[60] Analysis of data relating to litigation before the WTO shows that developing nations may not have improved their ability to operate effectively in the new system. Figures suggest that not only do developing nations use the Dispute Settlement Understanding less than equivalent procedures under GATT[61] but that they are less likely to bring complaints against developed nations than they were under GATT.[62] There are many reasons for this reluctance to file complaints. The main problem is perhaps the tendency to not make use of formal mechanisms. These issues will be exacerbated in the future with the problems stemming from GMO food and TRIPs. To refer back to the point made in the introduction to this chapter, this brief history of adjudication suggests that the economic determinants are more useful in explaining the fate of developing nations in world trade than the operation of either formal or informal "legal" relationships.

We need to carry these observations forward into a broader consideration of GATT/WTO.

Developing Nations and the GATT

GATT is marked by the way in which it handles the notion of the exception. We need to examine the general structure of GATT before turning to the provisions that relate to the economies of developing countries. It is worth noting, first of all, that the commitment to regular negotiation in article 28 is key to the operation of this regime: "there is no doubt that the periodic convening of the contracting parties of

GATT for detailed negotiation of the conditions of international trade has become a fundamental ingredient of the law of international trade."[63] The principles of world trade law are to be developed and implemented through a negotiating process. Once again, this must be distinguished from a more conventional constitutional legal structure, separated into legislative, executive, and judicial arms. Indeed, it is futile to look for such a "legal" basis, which must be found, instead, in a structure produced by the interrelation of legal and economic principles.

Article 1 (as amended) outlines one of the key provisions: the notion of the General Most Favored Nation. This lays down a requirement that "tariffs must be noncompetitive."[64] The article concerns the terms on which goods considered "like products" are to be traded. If a product is so considered, then it must be traded on equal terms with all trading partners. Thus, if there are duties, charges, or tariffs levied on that item, or if there are any privileges or immunities in relation to import or export, they must apply on equal terms to all "like products" that are traded with contracting parties.

The second major set of principles laid out in article 2 prevents increased trade barriers by limiting government restrictions on imports and exports and by committing nations to a regime of mutual controls on the movement of goods.[65] The so-called national treatment provisions in article 3 back this up.[66] Any discrimination against imported or "domestic products" in such a way as to offer protection to those products (for example, through "internal qualitative regulations") is prohibited. Article 7 details how goods are to be valued for customs purposes as a percentage of value. Duties imposed by governments are limited to tariffs levied on the importer. Other revenue mechanisms are forbidden. Quotas and licenses are not acceptable, unless they fall under a legitimate exception.

Developing nations are located in this structure through exemptions from and qualifications to the primary normative regime. So, in terms of the constitutional structure of the agreement, the "escape clause" (article 19) is vital. In the event of "unforeseen developments," this article allows the imposition of conditions on imported products. Likewise, conditions under 25.5 allow, in "exceptional conditions," the contracting parties to "waive an obligation" imposed by the agreement.[67] One might suggest that the determination of the exception is integral to the "sovereignty" of GATT. Indeed, commentators have argued that the very idea of the qualification or the exception is a key feature of the legal regime and that this has allowed "nondiscrimination" and the coordination of the "reduction of trade barriers" to become acceptable to such a large grouping of nations.[68] Historically, the exceptions to article 1 represent a compromise between the United States and the old colonial powers who wished to maintain the preferential links they had with their colonial or former colonial territories.[69] These preferences are no longer central to the operation of world trade. The major article creating exceptions is article 18.

Problems with article 18 can be traced to the drafting stage, where the specific difficulties faced by non-Western nations were noted, but no "deviation" from the general principles was countenanced.[70] Article 18 states that to raise the standard of living through economic development projects, a government may have to make recourse to "protective measures." These could include "flexibility" in tariff structures, to allow the development of a "particular industry," and "quantitative restrictions for balance of payment purposes." If a measure falls within these categories, a member may be allowed "to deviate temporarily" from the requirements of the GATT.[71]

How does this article create a set of provisions that apply to developing nations? It applies to economies that are in "early stages of development" and are only able to support "low standards of living" (annex I). An economy in "early stages of development" could be understood as one attempting to diversify and move away from "an excessive dependence on primary production." One commentator informs us that "Ceylon qualified under both criteria; its GDP was very substantially below that of Western Europe." As far as the second criterion was concerned, the proportion of the economy devoted to "manufacturing, mining and construction" must be "about ten percent."[72] If one ignores arguments about the accuracy of the comparators, it might be possible to gloss this definition as describing a structural weakness in a nation's economy that is persistent and fundamental.

How are these provisions developed? In the second paragraph, developing nations are described as relying on "export earnings." Not only is there the need for active policy, as outlined by paragraph d, but a legal order must be put in place as well. It is only when international trade is "governed by . . . rules and procedures" that operate in tandem with economic objectives that underdevelopment can be tackled. What are the precise measures that will be adopted? First of all there, must be a "rapid expansion of export earnings." Second, and begging the issue of its relation to this first objective, economic development depends on "diversification" so that developing nations are not limited to export of primary products. Developing nations thus require assistance with manufacturing and the opening of the markets on terms whereby they can compete fairly. This process envisages not only the ongoing provision of loan finance and coordination with the United Nations but also, most important, a qualification in the idea of reciprocity.

This takes us to the issue of the positing of developing nations in GATT's framework. Ongoing problems with the position of developing nations in world trade led to the location of the development mission within the general framework of GATT through the promulgation of Part IV, which came into effect in 1966. The key articles are 36, 37, and 38.[73] These articles provide measures that encourage export earnings, assist access to markets, and make financial help available. As part of this development package, article 36 can exclude developing nations from the obligations of reciprocity. But to what extent can any of these measures be enforced? Rights are nothing without the corresponding duties, and article 37 goes on to detail what obligations developed nations will assume. Of course, this is immediately qualified. Obligations will be honored "except for compelling reasons" not to do so. Such obligations extend to according "high priority" to lowering duties and tariffs that relate to exports to developing nations and to take similar measure in relation to fiscal measures that would "hamper" the "growth of consumption of primary products . . . in the territories of less developed countries."

On the whole, this raft of measures should not be seen as a major alteration of the fundamental GATT regime.[74] Indeed, after the promulgation of the development mission, balance-of-payment difficulties increased. There seemed to be a de facto mutation of GATT's scrutiny policies, as it was accepted that, rather than see periodic review as an opportunity to lift restrictions, it was necessary simply to keep such restrictions in place.[75] There were also fears that a "two-tier" GATT might be developing, with formalities insisted upon for developing nations but not for developed nations. We need to relate these themes to another essential feature of the GATT regime: the practice of negotiations between nations.

The Negotiating Rounds

In 1958, an action program was announced at the thirteenth session of GATT. The program was founded on the notion that developing nations would have to be treated differently and that notions of reciprocity and trade liberalization would have to be reviewed if there was to be economic recovery in the South.[76] In the Dillon round, though, these principles were rejected. The doctrine of reciprocity was reaffirmed, and it was noted that concessions had already been made under article 28 (bis).[77] The Tokyo round ran from 1972 until 1979 and can be seen as representing a further shift in policy toward developing nations. Once again, the overall objectives were affirmed as "mutual advantage, mutual commitment and overall reciprocity,"[78] and the notion of *most favored nation* (MFN) was stressed as a guiding concern.[79] During the ongoing negotiations, the Declaration of the New Economic Order strengthened the hands of developing nations with a coordinated call for the development of a trade regime that would be sympathetic to their needs. However, this group of nations, with the exception of Argentina, appeared to boycott the final signing of the agreement, in protest of their marginalization.[80]

In the wake of the Tokyo round, problems intensified. This was due to the diversification of the agenda and also to the increasing membership of the GATT. An important innovation to deal with these difficulties was the promulgation of a number of separate codes containing detailed provisions on various matters. The codes allowed the expeditious creation of a broader framework and a negotiating position where advantages and disadvantages for any particular nation could be balanced.[81] It also avoided detailed and time-consuming ratification provisions.[82] The question remained, though, of the precise status of those codes. As the codes did not create compulsory obligations, it appeared that the universal nature of GATT had been damaged because the codes allowed a qualification of the term MFN.

The critical question, however, is the extent to which the codes improved the negotiating position of less-developed nations, an issue that can be most usefully addressed directly after the Tokyo round. The United States agreed to a number of demands, and there were "Framework Agreements"[83] that suggested concessions, even if these had been won by splitting the solidarity of the less-developed nations. The agreements contained the celebrated "Enabling Clause," presented as an amendment to MFN status in article 1 and provided a legal framework for a number of measures covering preferential trade relations and "favorable treatment" for developing nations.[84] There were some tariff reductions, obtained without reciprocal concessions. However, this has to be seen in the context of the implementation of increasing restrictions placed on imports into developed nations that negatively affected export business.[85] Tokyo failed to determine a code of safeguards that would replace or clarify the inadequate provisions under article 19.[86]

The development of a regime of codes must also be seen as offering other problems and strategic possibilities. It is worth quoting Hudec on this point: "The code approach had very important implications for the legal relations between developed and developing countries. It proposed a new legal community, limited to those members who were willing to subscribe to the rules."[87] If the limited advances gained by developing nations were based on the creation of rules that acknowledged their difference as compared to developed nations and their requirement for special measures, the codes shifted the legal terrain. It made it necessary for structurally weak countries to begin bargaining from a position of formal equality. Misgivings of this nature, which focused on the need for subsidies, fed into the negotiation of specific provisions, Special and Differential Treatment for Developing Countries,[88] that relaxed the implementation of the codes in areas such as the Government Procurement Code.[89]

The Uruguay Round and the Birth of the WTO: A New Start?

The Uruguay round began in 1987–1988 and concluded in 1994.[90] There is insufficient space in this book to pursue many of these complex issues in depth,[91] so we will discuss in detail what has been described as "a new start for the international law of international trade":[92] the creation of the World Trade Organization.

The establishment of the WTO was integral to the elaboration of a framework for world trade that built on the principles of the GATT, although not all areas of economic or commercial activity fell within the regime. Importantly, the new system, as outlined in the following, built on certain ideas from the Tokyo round. The WTO was to have a dispute resolution mechanism and an impartial adjudicating body that would develop principles and would issue binding judgments.[93] The coherence of the system was further developed by the Trade Policy Review Body, offering the possibility of a proactive approach to problems bedeviling world trade, previously dealt with on a more or less ad hoc basis.

As the preamble to the agreement is relevant to the organization's autointerpretation, it is necessary to review it as part of a general inquiry into the constitutional structure of the WTO. As we are reading the document in its amended form after the Uruguay round of negotiations, it is not surprising that the reader encounters echoes of the other foundational documents that we considered in the previous chapter. Trade is depicted in the opening paragraph as being directed toward certain political and macroeconomic objectives: "raising standards of living," the maintenance of "full employment." The list of aims also covers the sustenance of international demand and, hence, income for the cooperating nations. However, the following clause is somewhat obscure. The first word, *while*, suggests that what follows coordinates what preceded it—that is, the previous sentence. Perhaps at this point, the tension between the various aspects of the WTO's mission is elided. Growth in real income and the continued expansion of world trade are placed against what could only be described as an "allowance," a gesture toward some concerns rather than a requirement or an obligation. The allowance is to use the "world's resources" efficiently along the lines of sustainable development with respect for the environment and to make allowances for nations at different stages of economic development.

Our concern here is with the privileging of a mission for development as a key concern of the WTO: a regard to the "developing countries" and, in particular, the "less developed amongst them." Here is the language of cooperation and sharing, a sense of the WTO as the great redistributor and coordinator of world commerce. How are these aims to be achieved? The third paragraph is explicit: the "reduction of tariffs" and "other barriers to trade" and, above all, the "elimination of discrimination" in global trading relations.

So, we can see that the WTO agreement provides a constitutional structure, a "common institutional framework" (article 2) binding on its members, through which trade is to be organized. The founding document gathers together "multilateral trade agreements" that are binding on members and "plurilateral agreements" that create obligations for those that are signatories but that are not binding on those members who have not accepted them. GATT 1998 is included into this network of treaties. The organization itself interacts with these treaties. Under article 3, the organization describes itself as a coordinating body that can administer the regime of rights and duties, offering itself as a negotiating body but, if necessary, implementing the commitments that have been made. Most important, we can see that this coordinating function extends to liaising with and ensuring coherence of policy with the IMF and the World Bank.[94]

Coda: The WTO after Cancun

Can we speak of any real improvements in the position of developing nations today?

WTO figures show that between 1990 and 2002, developing nations may have maintained their share of world trade, but they have remained on the margins of the world trade system as a whole. Although export earnings have grown (2002 showed a 4 percent growth to US$38 billion), imports have still exceeded exports (2002 showed an increase of 3 percent). A similar pattern emerges from the trade in services. Services trade accounts for roughly 20 percent of total world trade. For developing nations, however, this form of trade amounts to around 12.5 percent of total exports. Developing nations remain dependent on imports of commercial services, and their deficit in commercial services trade exceeds that of the deficit in merchandise trade.[95]

How has the WTO attempted to tackle this persistent problem of the marginalization of developing nations? Development was put firmly on the agenda in 1999 with the failure of the Seattle Ministerial Conference to agree on another round of talks. Seattle led to another questioning of the ability of the WTO to coordinate world trade; in particular, the consensus-orientated approach was criticized by developing nations. The WTO's own version of affairs contrasts this stalemate with the "breakthrough" that was achieved at the next ministerial meeting in Doha, Qatar, in 2001 with the promulgation of the Doha Development Agenda. This document affirmed the need for developing nations to achieve greater access in world markets and initiated a work program to push forward the development initiative. The programs concerned a declaration on objectives that had to be reached in negotiations in areas including intellectual property TRIPS, agriculture, industrial tariffs, and public health. Governance issues were also pointed up in concerns with governmental accountability. A second program was to focus on the problems of implementing WTO agreements in developing countries. The development agenda was also taken up in a ministerial acknowledgment of "the particular vulnerability of least-developed countries and the special structural difficulties they face in the global economy." Problems were to be practically addressed by increased contributions to technical support and capacity-building programs, coordinating with the efforts of partner institutions such as the IMF and the World Bank.

Most recently, at Cancun, Mexico, developing nations have shown a greater willingness to organize themselves into a power bloc. The Group of 21 is focused on Brazil, China, and India. There are a number of factors that have prompted the coming together of these nations. Opposition to the Multilateral Investment Agreement is founded on the argument that it will be a major qualification of national sovereignty and a further strengthening of international corporate power.[96] There is unrest over the inability to reach agreements over issues in agriculture, textiles, and human rights.

Less-developed countries are beginning to organize themselves around the issue of a more effective system of Special and Differential Treatment (SDT).[97] These agreements allow for special treatment for developing nations. Examples include extended time frames for the implementation of agreements, enhancing opportunities to increase the share of world trade, and assistance in the construction of infrastructure. This represents an intensification of the Doha agenda. There had been agreement that greater commitment was needed to SDTs; Cancun saw arguments that SDTs needed to be made into binding legal obligations. A total of eighty-eight proposals had been agreed on since Doha, and they were reclassified into a smaller number on which agreement could be reached; on the whole, though, it appeared that no overarching conclusion on the practice of SDTs had been reached.[98]

Cancun represents something of a turning point. Commentators have suggested that the collapse of the talks opens the possibility of a more democratic organization of world trade. Most recently, Brazil seems to have been emboldened by the aggressive position at Cancun in challenging U.S. cotton subsidies and European Union exports of sugar. Brazil is also calling for a further breaking down of protectionism and is continuing to resist the U.S. desire for regional free trade relationships. The major issue post-Cancun, then, is the extent to which we are witnessing a shift in the balance of power within world trade negotiations.

Conclusion

In our study of the IMF, the World Bank, and GATT/WTO, we have been grappling with an essential difficulty. Perhaps all our observations are symptoms of a wider problem, a difficulty that is attendant on the role of law in these international organizations. We are witnessing a breaking down of some of the certainties of conventional jurisprudence. In the place of the old order are regulatory regimes that operate along political or economic lines rather than in conformity with the logic of the law. Weil has described this system as one of inbuilt pathologies, a crumbling of the "conceptual scaffolding" required by the jurist.[99] If the "shifting" of international law away from concepts like sovereignty made for any substantive "transformation of relationships," then this could be applauded. We are, however, left in a world where some nations are more equal than others; in this sense, we are left in the worst of every possible world.

In the place of a legal regime that coherently lays out rules and the consequences that flow from their breach, there is a regime where the rules that structure economy are in the hands of powerful international agencies that are not adequately transparent. Risking generalization, there is a real sense in which the rule of law has either broken down or become a doctrine whose articulation appears to suit the prevailing economic order. At the same time, there is a danger of falling into despair. For some strong spirits, the international legal order opens new possibilities. This brave concern could be linked to a pervasive theme of this book. If there is to be a just international order, perhaps there is a need to redefine the very terms of international economic law. Marking recent scholarship in this area is the belief in the transformative power of human rights.[100] To affirm human rights is not to accept without question the ideology that links rights to the market. It is to suggest a slightly different development. If human rights were more central to the agendas of the IMF, the World Bank, and the WTO, then there would be a greater chance that a meaningful development agenda could be pushed forward. A recent UN subcommission report was critical of the role of the World Bank and other international lenders. The report proposes that if an action of a bank has resulted in "the exacerbation of poverty, a diminution of standards of livelihood, and a further distortion of existing social and global imbalances," then there should be a means to seek legal redress against such institutions.[101] Such developments return us to the problematic of hard and soft law that has been at the heart of this chapter. It may be that the dispossessed, the wretched of the earth, could be assisted by such a legal regime, by such an intervention by law into economy. Perhaps it would be possible to imagine a form of international economic law whose jurisprudence organized its concerns around the desire for a justice that privileged human dignity rather than for the efficient functioning, the smooth economy, of the world market.

Notes

1. The first attempts to produce an account of international economic law in the work of Erler and Schwarzenberger was focused on the need to discover underlying general principles. These included the principles of reciprocity, equal treatment, most favored nation, and fair treatment. It is worth noting that this scholarly exposition was also concerned with the legal status of developing nations. Alongside this regime of the equal application of general principles was the recognition of the need for preferential treatment, or the interruption of these general principles by the need to make provision for the nations of the developing world. Both developing and developed nations operate in a context produced by international law.

2. Two issues of definition need to addressed. In this chapter, and indeed throughout this book, *regulation* is meant in the sense of a mechanism that brings together hard law and other soft law and discretionary practices. For a useful introduction to the area of law and regulation, see G. Majone, *Regulating Europe* (London: Routledge, 1996), especially chapters 1 and 2 and the references to the wider literature. The issue of soft law also needs to be elaborated. How can we understand the idea of soft law? A useful starting point is through Joseph Gold, "Strengthening the Soft International Law of Exchange Arrangements," *American Journal of International Law* 77 (1983): 443–89. Summarizing the work of Seidl-Hohenveldern, Gold suggests that the distinguishing

feature of soft law is the "intended vagueness" of its obligations and the remedies for their breach. It is perhaps synonymous with "guidelines" or "declarations of principle." However, Gold argues that nations will take this kind of law seriously; there is also a tendency for soft law to become "hard law" over time. Perhaps most important, at least from our perspective, soft law is characteristic of international institutions because "of the deep divisions among members" (444). It is as if the political consensus for hard law does not exist. Against Gold it would be possible to argue that soft law will continue to characterize international economic law, precisely because the area is characterized by irresolvable political tensions.

3. As Jayasuriya writes, the term *governance* is normally associated with the World Bank and the structural adjustment policies of the 1980s. The notion of governance grew out of the failure of previous reforms to achieve their objectives. Policymakers determined that this was due to manifold failures of the political and legal institutions within developing nations. In the words of a World Bank discussion paper, the failure of development programs was due to "lack of an adequate legal framework, weak financial and auditing systems, damaging discretionary interventions . . . [and] closed decision-making which increases risks of corruption and waste." Governance is thus based on the idea that development programs will only succeed if legal, auditing, and democratic mechanisms are put in place at the same time that development finance is made available. In the sense developed in this chapter, the notion of governance is broadened to suggest the framework that is a product of World Bank and IMF collaboration. See Kanishka Jayasuriya, "Globalization, Law, and the Transformation of Global Regulatory Governance," *Indiana Journal of Global Legal Studies* 6, no. 2 (Spring 1999): 425–55. For an articulate, critical approach to the notion of conditionality, see Sundhya Pahuja, "Technologies of Empire: IMF Conditionality and the Reinscription of the North/South Divide," *Leiden Journal of International Law* 13 (2000): 749–813.

4. Terms such as *developing world, Third World,* or *less developed nations* are all contentious. As one point of reference, we could make use of the WTO's understanding of a "least-developed country," which is based on a definition employed by the UN. At present (2002) there are forty-nine least-developed countries on the UN list. Thirty of them are WTO members: Angola, Bangladesh, Benin, Burkina Faso, Burundi, Central African Republic, Chad, Democratic Republic of the Congo, Djibouti, Gambia, Guinea, Guinea Bissau, Haiti, Lesotho, Madagascar, Malawi, Maldives, Mali, Mauritania, Mozambique, Myanmar, Niger, Rwanda, Senegal, Sierra Leone, Solomon Islands, Tanzania, Togo, Uganda, and Zambia.

5. It must be noted, however, that there are those scholars who are skeptical of the very idea that there is an international monetary system. For instance, W. M. Scammell, *International Monetary Policy* (New York: Wiley,

1975), doubts whether the components for systemic functioning are present. It may be possible to have "knowledge, certainty and predictability" of the monetary system but not through any hard and fast laws. As Gold suggests, though, a useful place to start would be to consider the *Annual Report of the Fund for 1965* to consider how the IMF conceptualizes the problem. The system is seen as consisting of a "spectrum of customary institutional and legal arrangements which govern the conduct of international economic transactions, the methods of financing deficits and surpluses in international payments, and the manner in which countries are expected to respond to such deficits and surpluses." See Joseph Gold, "Legal and Institutional Aspects of the International Monetary System," *Selected Essays*, vol. 2 (Washington, D.C.: IMF, 1984), 48. In broadest summary, the fund defines the system as "a fair and efficient method of conducting international transactions." Without necessarily following Gold's conclusions about a definition of system, we might suggest that we are considering a system to the extent that we are concerned with relationships among institutions that attempt to operate in a coordinated manner.

6. Gold, "Legal and Institutional Aspects," 48. Gold argues that convertibility is a "crucial element in the international monetary system, the province of the Fund, and international monetary law" (168).

7. Article 1 can thus be seen as an interpretative framework; see F. A. Mann, *The Legal Aspect of Money, with Special Reference to Comparative Private and Public International Law* (Oxford: Clarendon Press; New York: Oxford University Press, 1992), 512.

8. Andreas F. Lowenfeld, *International Economic Law* (Oxford: Oxford University Press, 2002), 507.

9. Mann, *Legal Aspect of Money*, 515.

10. Mann, *Legal Aspect of Money*, 515.

11. See, for instance, Alexandre Kafka, "The IMF: Reform without Reconstruction," *Essays in International Finance* (Princeton, N.J.: Princeton University Press, 1976), 118, cited in Lowenfeld, *International Economic Law*, 535.

12. Asif H. Qureshi, *International Economic Law* (London: Sweet & Maxwell, 1999), 131.

13. Mann, *Legal Aspect of Money*, 507.

14. Lowenfeld, *International Economic Law*, 536.

15. Mann suggests that the definition of *capital* and *current transactions* provided by article 19.1 is problematic (see Mann, *Legal Aspect of Money*, 520).

16. Lowenfeld, *International Economic Law*, 508.

17. Mann, *Legal Aspect of Money*, 515.

18. Lowenfeld, *International Economic Law*, 509.

19. Lowenfeld, *International Economic Law*, 142–46.

20. Lowenfeld, *International Economic Law*, 509.

21. Quereshi, *International Economic Law*, 151 (quoting IMF articles).

22. Quereshi, *International Economic Law*, 142.

23. In the words of the IMF itself, "the financial assistance provided by the IMF enables countries to rebuild their international reserves, stabilize their currencies, and continue paying for imports without having to impose trade restrictions or capital controls. Unlike development banks, the IMF does not lend for specific projects." See www.imf.org/external/np/exr/facts/howlend .htm. More concretely, when a member state of the IMF is experiencing balance-of-payment difficulties, it can purchase foreign currency from the IMF using its own currency.

24. Lowenfeld, *International Economic Law,* 511.

25. Lowenfeld, *International Economic Law*, 513. At this period in the development of the IMF, the United Kingdom envisaged itself as a debtor nation, the United States as a creditor nation. The term *debtor nation* had yet to be associated with developing nations.

26. Lowenfeld, *International Economic Law*, 514.

27. See www.imf.org/external/np/exr/facts/conditio.htm.

28. Quereshi, *International Economic Law*, 190. There has been a certain degree of controversy over the precise legal status of the drawings from the IMF. IMF lawyers had refused to characterize a borrowing as a loan, even though, from the perspective of economics, the transaction does have this effect. However, in recent times the jurisprudence of the IMF has become more settled: a drawing can probably be seen as both a loan and an international agreement.

29. Quereshi, *International Economic Law*, 198.

30. Erik Denters, *Law and Policy of IMF Conditionality* (The Hague: Kluwer Law International, 1996), 22.

31. Denters, *Law and Policy*, 27.

32. Denters, *Law and Policy*, 27.

33. See Joseph Gold, *The Rule of Law in the International Monetary Fund*, IMF Pamphlet Series 32 (Washington, D.C.: IMF, 1980). See also, Denters, *Law and Policy*, 97.

34. Lowenfeld, *International Economic Law,* 546.

35. Lowenfeld, *International Economic Law*, 549–50. For a broader analysis of the economic reasons for the indebtedness of the developing world, see George McKenzie and Stephen Thomas, *Financial Instability and the International Debt Problem* (London: Macmillan). McKenzie and Thomas argue that the "fragility" of the market in general and the financial markets in particular has been underestimated in economic theory and exacerbated by free market policies. Free market reforms were an incorrect response to the unsustainable rise in the availability of credit earlier in the decade. Prompting the crisis was a fall in the income of developing countries while debt repayments increased.

36. Lowenfeld, *International Economic Law*, 550.

37. Lowenfeld, *International Economic Law*, 554–55. The PRGF can be seen as a form of "concessional lending" that makes funds available for economic growth; the HIPC, on the other hand, provides "debt relief" and relates to a nation's "external debt position." See International Monetary Fund, *Financial Organization and Operations of the IMF*, Pamphlet Series 45 (Washington, D.C.: IMF, 2001), 117.

38. Lowenfeld, *International Economic Law*, 555. For an analysis of the problem of debt from a perspective of sub-Saharan Africa, see George C. Abbott, *Debt Relief and Sustainable Development in Sub-Saharan Africa* (Brookfield, Vt.: Elgar, 1993). Generalizing about the situation as it stood at the end of the 1980s, Abbott writes that "poverty, ill-health, malnutrition and food insecurity . . . have all worsened. . . . The number of people facing food insecurity now exceeds 100 million." His figures are drawn from World Bank, *Sub-Saharan Africa* (Washington, D.C.: World Bank, 1989), 2–30.

39. New guidelines were issued for conditionality in September 2002. They detail "several interrelated principles" that stress that policy reform must be initiated and conducted at a national level and must be specifically addressed to the borrower's needs. See www.imf.org/External/np/pdr/cond/2003/eng/050803.htm.

40. See Denters, *Law and Policy*, 155.

41. Denters, *Law and Policy*, 17.

42. It is necessary to clarify two further preliminary concerns. The issue that we are focused on is not private debt but official debt, the debt of nations to the World Bank. It is also impossible to discuss loans to nations by commercial banks, simply through limitations of space. Furthermore, it is worth noting that there can be no recourse to bankruptcy law in this international area, as there is in a domestic situation. See Sigrun Skogly, *The Human Rights Obligations of the World Bank and the IMF* (London: Cavendish, 2001), 327.

43. From http://web.worldbank.org/wbsite/external/news.

44. Ibrahim Shihata, *The World Bank in a Changing World*, vol. 3 (The Hague: Martinus Nijhoff), 344.

45. Shihata, *World Bank*, 340.

46. Shihata, *World Bank*, 341.

47. Shihata, *World Bank*, 342.

48. Shihata, *World Bank*, 343.

49. Shihata, *World Bank*, 345

50. Shihata, *World Bank*, 350.

51. Kenneth W. Dam, *The GATT: Law and International Economic Organization* (Chicago: University of Chicago Press, 1970), 10.

52. John H. Jackson, *World Trade and the Law of GATT: A Legal Analysis of the General Agreement on Tariffs and Trade* (Indianapolis, Ind.: Bobbs-Merrill, 1969), 12.

53. Dam, *GATT*, 3.

54. Jackson, *World Trade*, 16.

55. Jackson, *World Trade*, 17.

56. Claude E. Barfield, *Free Trade, Sovereignty, Democracy: The Future of the World Trade Organization* (Washington, D.C.: AEI Press, 2001), 24.

57. Robert E. Hudec, *Developing Countries in the GATT Legal System* (Aldershot, Eng.: Gower, 1987), 77.

58. Hudec, *Developing Countries*, 80–81.

59. Barfield, *Free Trade*, 25.

60. Barfield, *Free Trade*, 25 (quoting Hudec).

61. Barfield, *Free Trade*, 25 (quoting Hudec). In the period 1995–2000, 29 percent of WTO complaints were brought by developing nations. Developing nations represent 80 percent of the WTO's membership.

62. Barfield, *Free Trade*, 25 (quoting Eric Reinhardt with Marc L. Busch). Reinhardt and Busch's analysis suggests that developing nations are one-third less likely to file complaints than they had been under the GATT system after 1989 (35). See E. Reinhardt and M. L. Busch, "Testing International Trade Law: Empirical Studies of the GATT/WTO Dispute Settlement," paper presented at the University of Minnesota Law School Conference on the Political Economy of International Trade, September 2000. See also Eric Rienhardt, *Aggressive Multilateralism: The Determinants of the GATT/WTO Dispute Initiation* (Atlanta, Ga.: Emory University, 2000).

63. Lowenfeld, *International Economic Law*, 30.

64. Bernhard M. Hoekman and Michael M. Kostecki, *The Political Economy of the World Trading System* (Oxford: Oxford University Press, 2001), 148.

65. Lowenfeld, *International Economic Law*, 28.

66. Lowenfeld, *International Economic Law*, 29.

67. Lowenfeld, *International Economic Law*, 41.

68. Lowenfeld, *International Economic Law*, 30–31.

69. Lowenfeld, *International Economic Law*, 31.

70. Jackson, *World Trade*, 628.

71. Dam, *GATT*, 10.

72. Jackson, *World Trade*, 652.

73. Jackson, *World Trade*, 646.

74. Robert E. Hudec, *Developing Countries in the GATT Legal System* (London: Trade Policy Research Centre, 1987), 28.

75. Hudec, *Developing Countries*, 33.

76. Hudec, *Developing Countries*, 42.

77. Hudec, *Developing Countries*, 42.

78. Lowenfeld, *International Economic Law*, quoting the declaration of the Ministerial Meeting, Tokyo, September 1973, GATT BISD, 20th Supp. 19 (1974).

79. Lowenfeld, *International Economic Law*, 55.

80. Lowenfeld, *International Economic Law*, 58.

81. Lowenfeld, *International Economic Law*, 57.

82. Hudec, *Developing Countries*, 84.

83. Hudec, *Developing Countries*, 84.

84. Hudec, *Developing Countries*, 85.

85. Hudec, *Developing Countries*, 76.

86. Lowenfeld, *International Economic Law*, 59.

87. Hudec, *Developing Countries*, 83.

88. Hudec, *Developing Countries*, 86.

89. Hudec, *Developing Countries*, 87.

90. Arguments over agriculture pitted the United States against Europe and also saw developing nations use arguments about protectionism in European farming as bargaining chips for opening their own markets to various new investment initiatives.

91. We will have to leave aside therefore any detailed consideration of the dispute resolution system that came out of the Uruguay round. Its main features are a unification of the mechanisms put in place in Tokyo and the creation of an appellate body. The system has also been streamlined in an attempt to resolve the delays that had bedeviled the previous system.

92. Lowenfeld, *International Economic Law*, 69. But see also, John H. Jackson and Alan O. Sykes, *Implementing the Uruguay Round* (Oxford: Clarendon Press, 1997). Reflecting on the conclusion of the round, the authors offer some interesting observations on the way in which the GATT/WTO is perceived by different countries. Developing nations tend to see the WTO as less interventionist than the World Bank and IMF. Developed nations and the EU are the greatest opponents to any increase in power of the WTO. The latter group is accustomed to "greater flexibility in international economic relationships" (467). Ultimately, concerns over sovereignty are dismissed as "silly"; the benefits of a coordinated system of world trade outweigh any compromises in areas where nations had traditionally claimed exclusive jurisdiction.

93. Lowenfeld, *International Economic Law*, 71.

94. In this context, the concept of a legal "interface" may be useful. See Christopher Arup, *The New World Trade Organization Agreements* (Cambridge: Cambridge University Press, 2000), Arup develops the notion of the interface to describe the way in which different "legalities" are linked together without necessarily being integrated.

95. Cancun press briefing at http://web.worldbank.org/wbsite/external/news/0,,contentmdk:20126037~menupk: 34465~pagepk:64003015~pipk:64003012~thesitepk:4607,00.html.

96. Fiona Macmillan, "If Not This World Trade Organisation, Then What?" *International Trade Law and Regulation* 3 (2004): 41–49.

97. Macmillan, "If Not This?"

98. Cancun press briefing (see note 95).

99. Prosper Weil, "Towards Relative Normativity in International Law?" *American Journal of International Law* 77 (1983): 413–41, 441.

100. And, indeed, the whole issue of "linkages" between different areas of law. See "Symposium on the Boundaries of the WTO," *American Journal of International Law* 96 (2002).

101. Quoted in Dana L. Clark, "The World Bank and Human Rights: The Need for Greater Accountability," *Harvard Human Rights Journal* 15 (2002): 225. See also, Korinna Horta, "Rhetoric and Reality: Human Rights and the World Bank," *Harvard Human Rights Journal* 15 (2002): 228–43.

THE CONTINUING IMPASSE: A GENEALOGY OF DEVELOPMENT LAW

Development law is founded on an inability to resolve the contradictions that brought it into the world.[1] Development law does not itself develop; rather, it circles around a fundamental problematic that it can articulate but not resolve. This is not to pillory development theory nor to argue that the rearticulations of the development "mission" may not have a positive impact. It is to suggest that development law cannot be thought of as a science or as a body of thought that reaches beyond its own ideological beginnings. Development law is thus a paradigmatic instance of the ideological disturbances that Steger associates with globalization.

This chapter shows that development law is a remarkably self-reflexive and mobile body of work. We will take as a major theme, the notion of the "impasse," or the interruption of development discourse, which in turn functions as a breach around which development law recomposes itself. What, then, is the moment of interruption? What impasse defines the subject?

We can trace two parallel and supporting critical interruptions in development law. These critical moments are an intervention that drew on varieties of Marxist theory and the campaign for a new international economic order (NIEO). In particular, this latter interruption remains ghostly or inchoate, a revelation of the possibilities of international law and an alternative notion of development. Even if the ultimate assessment of the NIEO is that it failed to produce any meaningful reorganization of world order, it represents the conclusion of a particular phase of development thinking and the opening of the present discourse on the right to development, sustainability, and human rights. After examining these terms, we will move toward the most recent arguments for restructuring international institutions and proposals for a tax on foreign exchange transactions to fund development. We will see that the structures of development law remain embroiled in the most profound ideological disagreements. Perhaps the final word is that we should not expect a subject that is so bound up with the political to have a neat, doctrinal coherence. Presenting the subject as anything more than an agonistic is to be blind to the porosity and disturbance that continue to characterize even development law's most recent manifestations.

Theories of Development

As an introduction to development law, it might be possible to suggest that its theoretical foundations are divided between a reliance on dependency theory and claims that rooted law in the need for modernization. Although this may appear a crude reduction of the positions in the development field as a whole, it is a useful way of describing the competing articulations of the role of the law. Such a distinction also helps us to position the critical impasse.

Modernization theory draws on the sociology of law. In particular, it builds on Weber's insight that law's rational organization of economy is essential for a modern, industrial society. Law makes for predictable decisions that, in turn, allow economic relations to be regulated and disputes determined. In Trubeck's articulation, law is "primarily a system of rules; it is a form of purposive social action, simultaneously part of, yet autonomous from, the nation state."[2] This legal order can be exported for the benefit of developing nations. Modernization theory thus makes an essential link between economy and law as a prerequisite for stable and sustainable growth. Consider the following example, drawn from an essay arguing for the need to create a new legal structure in Uganda:

> So long as the farmers, because of complex tribal, familial, or other institutions, do not have legal title, they cannot generate credit from lending institutions for agricultural modernisation. Therefore, although a Ugandan land tenure law ranks high on Kampala's agenda, it would be useless for politicians and draftsmen to sit down and write a new land title act.[3]

This is an argument that tries to balance the old and the new. The particularistic nature of tribal law contrasts with Western law; it varies from place to place in keeping with the mores of different tribes, clans, and families. Western law cannot simply be imposed. Experts must harmonize the two systems and show that modern law is the prerequisite for a system of land holding that can allow agricultural development.[4]

So, modernization theory must be understood as sensitive and flexible. For instance, Thomas M. Franck's work on "the new development" argues that the earlier theories of the subject had been too narrow and simplistic, imposing First World patterns on developing nations. Indeed, the new development is a movement away from law as a body of rules.[5] Law is socially rooted and essential to the normal functioning of any society.[6] For all this self-reflection, though, the new development does offer (no matter how qualified) a teleological model of development based on the historical experience of the United States. This model is based on a pattern that runs through unification to industrialization and social welfare.[7] In relation to this last stage, the work of the law and lawyers is central to "a new national system of norms and values."[8] Law is essential to the construction of a unified community where people participate in politics and public life.

It is not as if this approach is entirely out of step with certain contemporary features of development discourse. For instance, the new development argues that it is necessary to move away from gross domestic product as an indicator of progress. New development also stresses the importance of community (lawyers are particularly suited to this work because they can "promote reciprocity" and design a social system that has mass support because it is seen to be fair). But for all this commitment to these values, the new development is a "joint venture" between the United States and those who seek to join with it, a "mutual" compact between the developed and the developing worlds.

91

These assumptions about the development process were challenged from a variety of perspectives. One common point of criticism was the assertion that undeveloped societies could become developed through the assistance of Western technological expertise or the imposition of institutions modeled on those of the developed world. Such an approach ignores the different contexts and histories of "traditional" societies. The new development was also charged with a failure to understand that the disjunctures between the developed and the undeveloped were a product of the systemic operations of world economy. Undeveloped nations could not simply be abstracted from their position in world economy. Indeed, the very distinction between developed and undeveloped nations assumed that the latter were already "outside" of the structures that had produced prosperity for the First World, whereas their poverty could be accounted for more accurately by their subordinate location within world economy.[9]

A more radical analysis would begin with a distinction between developed metropole and undeveloped satellites. This division is based on a global division of labor and a requirement that production is for the market.[10] To borrow the language of Baran, the "unilateral transfers" of wealth from the colonized nations to those of Western Europe can be seen as a primary reason why intense industrial development in First World nations was accompanied by the traumatic dislocation of agricultural societies forced to service the requirements of their colonial masters.[11] This interference in the process of capital accumulation could be seen as having a serious impact on the development of the colonized territories.[12]

A total critique of the very terms in which the modernization framework operates can be found in Wallerstein's world systems theory.[13] The underpinnings of the disequilibria in world economy can be related to the interaction of certain key factors. World economy can be seen as a product of the geographical expansion of Western power from the sixteenth century onward. This process is coupled with a zoning of the world, a specialization of different areas in the production of materials and labor for manufacture. In turn, this zoning relates to interactions between colonial expansion and economic development along capitalist lines. The process is accompanied by an institutional logic that locates the development of strong states at the center of economic networks that can ensure the ongoing transfer of resources to the developed economies.

It is somewhat clumsy to lump these differently nuanced accounts together and even more reductive to label them "dependency" theory. We will return to this point, but first it is worth noting that these forms of Marxist theory do contain insights about the role of the law as well as the functioning of economy.[14] Dependency theorists point out with reference to the historical record that the effects of legal reform did not evolve as the modernizers had depicted. Consider the example of Turkey. The founding of the republic in 1924 saw the abolition of sharia law and the promulgation of a legal system based on European models. Despite this legal modernization, there remain deep-seated problems in the Turkish economy, as evidenced in the application of the Turkish government to the IMF at the end of the 1980s. Consider two further examples: the legal reforms introduced by the Brazilian military after the coup in 1964 and the Chilean junta in 1973. These reforms were broadly along the lines proposed by modernization theorists, but as the poor economic development of those nations in the 1970s and 1980s suggests, legal and economic reform did not go hand in hand and were not mutually supporting.[15]

In summary, the record of legal modernization is a poor one. Perhaps what we find with this particular theory is an account "suited to American corporate penetration of the economies of the less developed countries in the context of state directed capitalisitic economic development."[16] From this perspective, the coups of the 1970s show an inescapable feature of the politics of legal modernization. Although it is risky to generalize, the following pattern can be observed. The overthrow of democratically elected governments was tolerable because the dictators that replaced them were also committed to a certain kind of economics. The military regimes were committed to forms of capital accumulation that served the interests of domestic elites and "dismantle[d] popular redistributive programmes."[17] It may have been possible to generate high profits in certain economic sectors, but this would have been at the cost of underdeveloping domestic markets and repealing "social" legislation, such as the minimum wage. Thus, one can see another feature of military regimes: the suppression of political dissent and the deterioration in standards of living.[18]

The New International Economic Order, or the Ghost in the House of Development Law

The NIEO emerged in a space defined by the political economy of dependency theory.

UNCTAD, the United Nations Conference on Trade and Development, was formed in 1964. In 1973, UNCTAD announced a declaration and a program of action to create a new international economic order. The NIEO should be seen as "the first or initial formulation of ideas based on an entirely different philosophy of development and international economic relations."[19]

The backdrop of the NIEO was one of failure: failure of GATT, the IMF, the World Bank, and the second decade of the United Nations development strategy.[20] The output of the poorest nations had grown only 2 percent in the 1973–1975 period, in comparison with a 4 percent rate of growth in the 1960s. Poorer nations were experiencing a steadily falling balance of trade and growing deficits. Exports of primary commodities were bringing in less revenue, and imports were costing more. The need to finance those deficits added to the problems of nations already servicing large debts. But as UNCTAD documents describe, those failures cannot just be seen as a problem of economics. They must be seen in a political context: "colonialism, foreign aggression and occupation, including apartheid, remain in many parts of the world."

UNCTAD saw this problem as one belonging to the developed nations, not to the developing nations. Solutions to problems of underdevelopment thus had to be found in the behavior of the developed nations who had failed to meet the targets set by the international development strategy. For instance, little progress had been made on GATT negotiations for the lifting of restrictions on the exports of primary and processed commodities from developing contracting members.[21] Although GATT had implemented a generalized system of preferences (GSPs) covering manufacturing, those preferences had been unduly restricted by the imposition of ceilings and other limitations. Developed nations thus effectively protected their own domestic markets against foreign competition.

The NIEO demanded a reappraisal of the institutions of the world order, affirming the centrality of "equity, sovereign equality, independence, interdependence, common interest and co-operation."[22] For the nations of the developing world, the NIEO laid down obligations that represented "a new standard."[23] We could place it alongside the Havana Charter, as this document also articulates an alternative vision of world trade. The Havana Charter explicitly returns to article 55 of the Charter of the United Nations and the demand for "full employment and conditions of economic and social progress and development." Nations, individually and collectively, pledged themselves to assist "those countries which are still in the early stages of industrial development." To those ends, article 15 specifies that "preferential agreements" between nations were justifiable. It would appear, then, that an alternative structuring of world trade was possible, arising from the UN rather than from an autonomous notion of free trade.

Developing nations considered that the charter contained binding obligations, basing their argument on article 56 of the UN Charter and resolution 2626.25. These provisions were interpreted as facilitating cooperation in the field of development, or "the realisation of economic and social rights."[24] The argument was supported by reference to the practice of the "juridical and political organs of the UN" to see these rights as hard law obligations. Further UN resolutions confirmed that the charter was coherent with the principles of international law, including the duty of states to cooperate with each other.

We need to follow the development of the NIEO. The draft of the Declaration on International Development submitted by the Soviet Union to the Economic and Social Council of the UN had the principles of the NIEO at its heart.[25] The document was aimed at the "equitable exchange of goods" among developing nations. It proposed certain agreements over the terms of international commodity trade and, most radically, the creation of a fund composed of financial resources resulting from disarmament, which could be utilized to assist development. However, the various working groups and drafting parties could not agree on a text and a form of words. The final version, the Statement of Principles for Governing International Trade Relations and Trade Policies Conducive to Development, with its fifteen general principles (issued in 1964), thus appeared as a palimpsest. The working group had failed to achieve consensus; it "decide[d]" to enclose in brackets the phrases on which agreement could not be reached.[26] This is perhaps the fate of a document that reveals trade as a site of contention over its legal and economic meanings. We seem a long way from the theories of eventual market resolution that underpin the dominant account of GATT. The nebulous legal status of the NIEO reflects the fact that its economics, and the terms in which it challenged the global order, could not be allowed to achieve a positive legal form. The NIEO occupies a spectral position in the margins of international economic law.

A Right to Development: The True Beginnings of Development Law?

The NIEO took a wrong turn. It was too enmeshed in the postcolonial struggle, incapable of compelling consent for its key principles. But, according to scholars and commentators on the international law of development, the mission continues. We must learn from past failure; we must create a body of development law that can open its arms to the world.

This new beginning draws on various sources. It makes use of the UN "Global Compact," various other charters, and the IFIS's perception of the development mission. Some bold claims have been made for the nature of this new subject. We should no longer talk of law *and* development. The "and" suggests an area of doctrine that has not yet come of age and remains an unfortunate hybrid. A new conceptualization of development law as a "paradigm" is required. Drawing on work in the theory of science, this argument suggests that the subject must be thought of as being a set of shared conventions that define the foundational problems that structure it as a discipline and allow its principled development.[27] Development law is thus providing itself with a "constitution";[28] a sense of clear foundations is emerging for the first time. What we appear to be witnessing, then, is the "true" birth of an objective body of development law that can be distinguished from the compromised and ideologically flawed versions that went before and spoke in its name.

So, this is a body of law that assumes a background in Western legal thought but "differs significantly" to the extent that it "does not stem from formal, imperial or military conquests."[29] It must be thought of as a professional body of knowledge, a science of aid, a "bridge" between the developing and developed worlds. More precisely, it connects those bodies of law that are of most assistance to developing nations, linking together bankruptcy law, company law, the law of investment, intellectual property, human rights, and environmental legislation. One can clearly see, then, that it is not new doctrine but a new conceptual linkage of existing bodies of doctrine. It stresses that development is not simply the preserve of sovereign states but that it involves many stakeholders; indeed, to the extent that the old adjectives are applicable, it is a public law based in part on private transactions.

These claims may seem somewhat overenthusiastic. However, even if one would not agree that development law could so easily depart from an ideological past and become a "science of aid," there is a sense in which the entire discourse is shifting. Our central question, though, will be whether or not this realignment is anything more than a new impasse. Claims that development is now a science sit unhappily alongside equally influential arguments that are associated with the creation of a right to development. There is also a return to notions of the state and the rule of law that, again, suggest the shifting terms that continue to make up development theory.[30]

In 1986 the General Assembly of the UN promulgated the right to development. The right is intended to resolve social, economic, and humanitarian problems and promote "human rights and fundamental freedoms." These objectives are associated with the International Covenant on Economic, Social, and Cultural Rights and the International Covenant on Civil and Political Rights. However, the right to development is given an explicit political edge by being linked to "decolonization" and to the rights of peoples to "self-determination." These claims are conjoined with the notion of development as a wide-ranging process, which is based on communal participation in economic, social, cultural, and political activity that results in an "fair distribution" of the "benefits" produced.

These claims echo and reinvent certain ideas that run through the NIEO. Perhaps the key theme is the notion of the interconnected and indivisible nature of all rights. In some ways, this is a departure from the dominant view. Conventional jurisprudence would consider that civil rights are legal rights that create obligations and duties. Social and economic rights relate to matters of policy and are thus unsuitable claims for the law. However, the right to development also moves on from the NIEO. Note that the "the central subject in the development process" is the "human person." This would seem to separate the right to development from key claims of the NIEO as it seeks to avoid any collectivist interpretation. We are individuals first and foremost, members of a collective in only a secondary sense. At the same time, we can see the influence of the NIEO on the language of this declaration in the linking of human rights to a "new international economic order"; the reaffirmation of sovereignty over natural resources; and the enumeration of apartheid, colonialism, and neocolonialism as "massive and flagrant violations of human rights."

These arguments and concerns also underlie the individual articles. Thus the "inalienable human right" to development of article 1 "entitle[s]" involvement in those activities that perpetuate material life. This right also covers self-determination and sovereignty over resources; and must be linked to the problem of regional secession as considered in chapter 2. The Nigerian civil war was fought over an issue of self-determination that was also a claim to sovereignty over the resources of a region that had found itself federalized at its own expense. It begs the wider question of whether the self-determination of ethnic groups has been dealt with in a principled manner by states of the developing world. Such unresolved issues perhaps haunt the right to development.

Article 2 restates the centrality of the human being to the development process. This right presents the human being as an individual rooted in a political community that should be organized toward an end that best realizes equitable distribution. Is there a sense that the politically sovereign states created in the struggle against colonialism have failed to create and sustain democratic cultures? Article 3 operates at an international level, again recalling the NIEO's call for mutual aid and cooperation between nations. This call is extended in article 4 to the duty to collaborate on international development plans, and the call is extended still further in article 7 to cover disarmament.

So, the right to development can be seen as a document that potentially challenges both the developing and the developed world but carries within it a certain irresolution. If we take it at face value, we can see that the development mission is recomposed around a political problem that is challenging for a postcolonial order that has seen governmental elites entrench themselves and a wide scale failure of democratic culture.[31]

This orientates the debate firmly toward a new political problematic. Indeed, this runs through the so-called basic needs approach that developed by reference to the right. The basic needs approach presents development as something that cannot just be assessed in terms of gross national product. Development is related to an idea of "human need" that is translated into legal claims to economic and social rights.[32] Poverty, as a deprivation of these essential rights, is understood as a structural problem. In part, this has to do with the location of less-developed countries in the world economy. But problems also stem from the rules of international law. These rules serve to articulate law in terms of independent state entities and sovereign governments. Law should address the complex interrelationships between the actions of developed states, powerful multinational corporations, and governmental elites in the developing nations themselves. If law begins from this nexus, it can begin to tackle the structural nature of poverty and underdevelopment.

The basic needs approach appears agnostic toward the free market, arguing merely that, given certain political initiatives, the market can be tamed and operated beneficially. Human rights are central to this rethought economic and political order. Most succinctly, the state in developing nations is presented as "both a creditor and a debtor."[33] A developing nation is entitled to aid only to the extent that it honors and protects the human rights of its citizens. Relationships between states have to be perceived as integrally related to the state's internal relationships with its own "people." Thus, at the international level, the state is the "subject" of the right to development, while at the national level, this right is exercised by individuals and groups. Grounding this is the desire for a fundamental shift in the legal paradigm. Connecting the state's obligation as an "external" international actor with duties that it owes "internally" is an elaboration of a development law that might be able to make a claim to universal, humanitarian resonance.

But can we find with the right to development and the basic needs approach anything more than a more precise articulation of the ideological tensions of development? The basic needs approach is an impasse, as it produces another set of tensions rather than a resolution of the fraught political struggles that compose the field. Perhaps we need to acknowledge that the basic needs approach does recompose the problematic.

It cannot be dismissed as merely a rehashed version of Marxism/Leninism, nor can it be simply seen as the NIEO revisited. Indeed, there is a certain criticism of the underpinnings of the NIEO for privileging the sovereignty of developing nations above human rights obligations.[34]

This does not suggest that the basic needs approach has been universally accepted. Indeed, both basic needs and the right to development have been criticized as vague "third generation" rights. In turn, though, apologists for the basic needs approach have outlined the new thinking that is demanded from those who are too quick to condemn. Unless one acknowledges the existence of solidarity rights, then the state has no obligation to protect the basic needs of its citizens, and classical rights are meaningless. Indeed, third-generation rights can be seen as the very foundation of the classic rights and liberties. Inseparable from this is the need for a developing nation to have an impartial legal system committed to due process: "the access of the poor to legal services must be extended as an aspect of their active participation in development."[35] It appears, then, that the basic needs approach extends to the creation of a domestic political and legal culture as the very foundation of economic development. In this sense, the position is not incompatible with present World Bank policy on the rule of law. This, in turn, testifies to the way in which the basic needs approach is integratable with the visions of the dominant development community. We will follow this fault line presently.

Our critical questions about basic needs and the right to development need to be supplemented by a consideration of the sustainability approach. Sustainability is closely connected with elements of the basic needs project, but it also shifts the terrain of the debate. We will see that the discourse of ecological responsibility sponsored by the sustainability approach is another site of ideological struggle. Key principles are articulated in the work connected with the Brundtland Commission and the publication of the twenty-two articles. The discourse is organized around the need for an environment capable of providing "health and well-being," a demand that is a "fundamental" human right. This translates into a catalogue of duties imposed on the state to preserve the environment and to assess environmental change as part of economic development.[36] These duties have been criticized for containing too many implicit assumptions about economic development. A more carefully worked out statement can be found in the Draft International Covenant on Environment and Development of 1995, an elaboration of the Rio principles. Environmental and economic development are carefully articulated with reference to a "right" to development, which is linked with the need to end "unsustainable" patterns of economic growth.

Sustainability shares with stakeholder orientations a vision of development as a process in which all must collaborate and in which there needs to be participation by the relevant actors at a national and an international level. Environmental law addresses itself primarily to those industrialized nations responsible for pollution and the degradation of the global environment. Just as those nations have a responsibility to control their own consumption, poorer nations have a responsibility for the matters over which they have control, such as population growth. Although allowances can be made for the differential position of developing nations, environmental discourse shares with the basic needs approach the belief in common standards and universal application. These principles also return to the aspects of the NIEO that attempt to coordinate sovereignty over resources with a call for their equitable use and consumption.

It is not as if these initiatives in development law can mend the tensions that exist within the subject. Indeed, there are more radical critiques of this new phase of development thinking that make the link between "global environmentalism" and imperialism[37] or "ecological imperialism."[38] Indeed, in the wake of the Earth Summit, it is possible to point to a new nexus of concerns that bind sustainability and access to food, natural resources, and technology. To insist that this takes the form of neo-imperialism, though, is to try to disrupt "ecoliberal" notions of responsibility that underlie this entire field. Usage and development of natural resources are now linked to a discourse that operates in terms of a notion of global responsibility. Affirming this responsibility is clearly going to interfere with the way in which governments of the developing world are able to use their own resources. There are some positive impacts on development practice that may be brought about by this sensitivity to the impact of industrialization. However, the point of the critique is that sustainability fails to identify the underlying reasons for underdevelopment in the first place.

Sustainability is related to the broader discourse of global survival that grew up in the period after the Second World War. The problem is seen in terms of an "internationalisation of the environment" that privileges a notion of a global ecosystem rather than that of "local cultures."[39] The critique problematizes the "we" that underlines sustainability rhetoric. On the surface this is an appeal to shared humanity, but underneath this claim to shared belonging is a return to the vision of social management that characterized the very beginnings of the development mission. Now, though, it is the discourse of sustainability, furthered by the World Bank and "mediated by Gro Harlem Bruntland, the matriarch scientist" that provides the substance of an argument that aims to reconcile the demands of development and the sustenance of natural resources.

The discourse of ecology is also bound up with economics, or, rather, with the "dominant economic worldview."[40] Notions of planning and the objectivity of a science that can produce neutral findings about the world are brought together in a new conjugation, but what remains the same is the way that the developing world is made the subject of these processes. Indeed, this coordinates with the broader understanding of the "impasse" of development theory: "the sustainable development discourse redistributes many of the concerns of classical development."[41] In this sense the basic needs approach and the sustainability approach merely alter the operating terms of the development discourse: the fundamental drive remains the same. They represent a "new technology of government."[42] The concerns of environmentalism, from this perspective, are ways in which people and processes can be monitored and controlled and turned into bodies of knowledge. The law plays an important role in this broader creation of structures of power/knowledge. The old distinction between binding law and voluntary codes is now more fluid; both are involved in creating objects of knowledge that can be policed and improved. Importantly, though, it is the very discourse of the global that effectively repositions Third World actors as subjects of global responsibility. We can relate this to the issue of "visibility," or the nature of the problems that eco-discourse isolates.[43] Eco-discourse tends to take the "degrading" activities of peasant farmers out of contexts that, when studied, suggest that the problem of the degradation of environment is caused by broader processes of development and by the dislocations and displacement of peoples that such processes cause. Thus, one risks placing the blame on peasant farmers for certain agricultural methods as opposed to placing it on the activities that make those methods necessary in the first place. The new discourse of ecology shifts the axis of responsibility from the developed to the developing world.

Coda

The final phase of this chapter describes how contemporary debates about development circle around issues such as human rights, governance, and the rule of law. As the development debate engages with these issues, the disputes about the nature of law and globalization may have shifted their terms, but the ideological disputes remain just as serious. We will look at the World Bank's repositing itself as a symptomatic issue.

The World Bank has adapted its position and incorporated a number of formally critical ideas into its understanding of the development mission. The World Bank has created a sophisticated, multifaceted discourse. Criticisms of the World Bank, in turn, have redefined themselves. An immanent critique of the bank's practices has shown itself to be possible, but more radical interventions have begun to question the very composition of the structures for debt and international movements of money. Perhaps we are again within a critical moment, similar to the emergence of the NIEO. At present it is too soon to say whether calls for a Tobin tax (detailed later in the chapter) or a new international body to oversee and regulate debt issues will lead to reforms. However, what does remain clear is that, despite the World Bank's flexibility and ability to respond to criticism, development law remains a deeply divided subject.

Of late the World Bank has increasingly defined its development mission around an articulation of human rights based on its critique of its past failures. The World Bank has admitted that there has been a gap between a commitment to human rights, as articulated in the Universal Declaration of Human Rights, and its own practices in implementing its programs.[44] The discourse presently favored redefines the debate on different generations of human rights. Policies are now effectively predicated on and do recognize second-generation rights. Thus, to the extent that projects are aimed at education, health care, food security, sanitation, and housing, the bank is acknowledging the importance of these rights.[45] Moreover, rights are seen as "interconnected." This means that rights are dependent on civil society and a vigorous democratic culture. Rights culture is "both the design and the product of people organized through government." That rights bind together economy, government, and society can be shown through practical examples. Consider the issue of "public services." Public services can only operate if they are correctly targeted and provided by a transparent government that is not disabled by corruption. Rights of children and the legislation to protect these rights will be effective only in the social and economic conditions where parents can earn a decent wage. Finally, rights only make sense if there are courts and a functioning legal system to protect those rights.[46]

To take one final aspect of the World Bank's doctrine, we can see that a concern with gender has been positioned within doctrines of governance and human rights. A recent document presents gender mainstreaming as an issue of "developmental effectiveness";[47] gender is to be made central to the work of the bank and a key issue in the development of programs, allowing for a greater needs-specific targeting of lendings. Gender mainstreaming in areas such as health and education allows a greater sensitivity to the needs of disadvantaged women, but this initiative breaks into areas that have not normally been seen as being open to this kind of needs analysis, such as transport and energy.[48] Indeed, so central has gender become that it appears fundamentally linked to the very idea of economic growth and the movement of "men and women" out of poverty. More specifically, World Bank research has shown that the gender-based division of labor and disparities in power and entitlement "undermine economic growth."[49] In broadest outline, the remedial approach stresses "investment in human capital," primarily the health of women and girls, opening up financial resources to women, primarily through employment access to land and the "labour of other family members." Women are also seen to bear more critical attitudes toward corrupt government practices—and thus gender can also be associated with the need for transparent institutions.[50]

Possibilities for Critique

If the World Bank has proved itself flexible enough to adapt to the criticisms that have been made of its position, how can critique proceed?

One way would be to look at the very discourse of accountability that the World Bank has created and to ask whether it lives up to the ideals of transparency that it clearly sees as being so central to governance. We could look, first of all, at the composition of senior positions in the bank (and for this matter, the IMF). The problems with the transparency of selections procedure for senior figures notwithstanding, it is difficult to see why the two most senior positions are reserved for candidates from the United States and Europe. Why should candidates from the developing world be excluded? There are also significant issues in the gender composition of the senior management of the bank. In 2002, the board at the IMF had no female members, and the World Bank's board was 92 percent male.[51]

There is a similar pattern in the allocation of votes among board members. As the board wields great power in bank policy, this is another serious imbalance of power. A recent Christian Aid report illustrates this fact succinctly: "The U.S. is the only country with enough votes to block board decisions on its own. By contrast, the world's poorest countries cannot block a decision even if they all join together."[52] At present, voting rights are allocated by reference to "economic weight" that reflects the dominance of the founder-member, "industrialized" nations. However, if one looks at the present ways in which the World Bank raises finance, one would see a move away from the beneficence of the developed world to making use of financial markets and, to some extent, interest payments from loans to primarily middle-income countries. Moreover, if one allows for the increasing share of world output that comes from Asian countries, then the proportionate rise in economic weighting of these nations would demand a far greater representation at the bank's board level. Serious questions could also be asked about the way in which developing countries are represented. On the boards of both the IMF and the World Bank, two members represent forty-four African countries.

There are other issues. Significant problems remain with the transparency of decision-making processes that regulate projects in developing nations. One example is the Lesotho Highland Water Project. Work on the project had a serious impact on access to land and water for local peoples, and the amounts of compensation paid have been shown to be inadequate. How could these decisions and practices be scrutinized? Although the setting up of inspection panels in 1993 represents a useful initiative, there is no guarantee that they can provide a truly critical input, as the initiation of investigations rests with the executive board.[53] Furthermore, as there is still no obligation for board decisions to be published, it is impossible to bring any public pressure to bear on those who are making the decisions or even to monitor the precise terms in which decisions are made.[54] The implications of this lack of transparency extend to the fact that a decision of the World Bank not to make a loan may also influence the decisions of other lenders. When one considers the evidence that World Bank/IMF policy serves to undermine democratic institutions, one quickly sees how problems are compounded. In 2003, the Ghanaian government announced that it intended to increase import tariffs on rice and other foodstuffs in order to improve the livelihoods of farmers and to restrict subsidized imports from abroad. The increases were within the limits set by the WTO. However, the increases went against advice given by the IMF. Under pressure from IFIs, the Ghanaian government retracted its proposals, a decision that bypassed the Ghanaian parliament.

More radical critiques of IFI go beyond recommending reforms of the World Bank or IMF board structures and draw attention to the very organization of the international system of finance. We will look at issues surrounding debt to elaborate these themes. Critique begins from the assertion that the system has been designed by the world's wealthy nations. These complex themes will have to be dealt with at the level of crude summary. Consider the following argument.[55] Macroeconomic "cycles" make the system crisis-prone, as overextensions of credit lead to "slumps" that have negative effects on the economies of developing and developed countries. The entire practice of international borrowing needs to be reassessed. First, the present structure ignores the fact that there are two parties that are responsible for a loan, the creditor and the debtor. Through ideas developed in the U.S. bankruptcy code and the work of the Austrian economist Kunibert Raffer, it is possible to propose a more equitable structuring of the debt relationship. One has to remember that it is necessary for developing and developed countries to share the risks of debt—especially when loans are made to sovereign governments—but that the effects of the debt crisis are felt by the populations of developing nations.[56]

This would go much further than would the proposals of the IMF for a sovereign debt-restructuring mechanism, as the latter does not take into account the responsibility that the creditors must bear for encouraging lending in the first place. As there is no independent scrutiny of the IMF, the fund becomes the arbitrator in its own cause. Any economic restructuring would thus reflect the goals of the IMF or its powerful backers. In a 2003 meeting in Washington, D.C., proposals were mooted that would allow for punitive measures to be taken against debtors if they were to agree with other creditors to terms that were seen by the IMF as being "too generous." What resources could be drawn upon to provide a rethinking of the situation? There is, arguably, a role for nongovernmental organizations (NGOs) and civil society groups in presenting arguments about the impact of debt. Furthermore, what could be learned from domestic bankruptcy law? In domestic law, the debtor draws up the plans for the restructuring of the debt. Could this provide a new model? Given this dynamic, a framework for international debt negotiation should be put in place.

Creating this network would build on ideas for the rule of law. Running through the criticisms outlined here is indeed the idea that international economic justice cannot be obtained while bodies such as the IMF sit as judges in their own causes. The other key principle is that the debts of sovereign bodies concern public money. If such public funds are involved, then there is a necessity for transparent and accountable institutions to be put in place. This could be achieved if an independent court was set up to adjudicate between the claims of debtor and creditor countries. The IMF would still have a role in organizing and providing finance, but the UN would also play a more central role in producing the analyses of sustainability. These proposals represent only one possible approach to the necessary redesign of international institutions. Other NGOs and pressure groups have called for the abolition of the IMF and the complete assumption of its duties by the UN. Other proposals suggest a far more informal body that would be "highly flexible" because the process of adjudication would remain in the hands of the parties involved (although it might be necessary to set up a small secretariat under the auspices of the UN).[57]

Other proposals for radical change have looked more toward adopting the Tobin tax rather than the creation of an international court (although, of course, one could imagine a program that would include both).[58] The Tobin tax is based on the work of the economist James Tobin, who argued for a tax on foreign exchange transactions so that it would operate like "sand in the wheels of currency speculation."[59] Essentially, then, the Tobin tax is a tax on the turnover of the foreign exchange market. The foreign exchange market sees vast movements of money; some estimates suggest that over one trillion dollars is traded every day. At first, the market existed to service foreign trade, but it has increasingly become rife with short-term investments, "hot money," and currency speculation, geared to the rapid realization of profit. These forms of currency dealing are detrimental to world trade and the economies of sovereign states. Recent history has also shown that currency speculation, primarily by Western banks, has caused immense damage to economies in Thailand, Indonesia, and Mexico.

If a small tax were levied on these transactions (much less than 1 percent), it is likely that it would generate a great deal of revenue, which could be directed toward development goals. At present there is no tax regime specific to the foreign exchange market. Banks do pay corporation tax on their profits, but there are no taxes as such on foreign exchange trading. Proposals for the implementation of the tax argue that it could operate at two levels. There would be a low rate to cover daily transactions and a higher rate that would be used to discourage attacks on currencies by speculators. Institutional reforms would be necessary: the body charged with implementing the task would have to be open and accountable and would probably operate under the authority of the UN. There would have to be a strong input from grassroots organizations to ensure that the revenues raised were deployed in the most effective ways.[60]

Rats and Government

It is illustrative of development theory's tensions that critics are now speaking of "a new dependency."[61] Although it is possible to see that development theory and development law have changed over time and made for different practices, there is a fundamental irresolution at the heart of the very discipline. This means that it is far too soon to speak of the maturity of law and development. Indeed, we need to see it as one of the many largely inchoate and provisional ways in which law is both a part of and a response to the agonistics of the global. We have argued that there are many aspects of this tension in development law. For instance, we were concerned with the NIEO as a kind of portal where different conceptions of law, rights, and global prerogatives emerge into the traditionally limited field of international law. The failure of the NIEO inspired the next movement forward, which redefined the field but was still vulnerable to the critique of those who see sustainability and basic needs as sophisticated operations of power. However, there are clearly exciting developments within this body of work, not least the attention on the human rights obligations of institutions such as the IMF. We are at present within the space where, as one of the major textbooks states, the focus of traditional human rights law has changed. We are in a problematic area where "economic analysis must supplement legal and policy analysis."[62] Development theory, then, has to be read as a volatile and shifting field whose very capacity for realignment, while preventing the subject from achieving coherence, offers possibilities for intervention and argument. In the name of humanity?

Notes

1. As a body of doctrine, development is clearly more than a discourse about law. In focusing on the juristic aspects of development, it is necessary to remember that this is merely a part of a much broader set of assumptions and practices; these concerns will have to remain on the edges of this present work that is necessarily limited in scope.

2. David M. Trubeck, "Towards a Social Theory of Law: An Essay on the Study of Law and Development," *Yale Law Journal* 28, no. 1 (1972): 42.

3. Thomas M. Franck, "The New Development: Can American Law and Legal Institutions Help Developing Countries?" *Wisconsin Law Review* 12:767–801, 799 (1969).

4. Rumu Sarkar, *Development Law and International Finance* (The Hague: Kluwer Law International, 2002). It would be wrong to argue that it is only a sociology of law that has influenced the increasing reliance on the rule of law in World Bank and IMF relief packages; however, if this theory of law is linked to the other exigencies and pragmatic influences that feed into the process of conditionality and structural adjustment, it may be possible to speak of a globalized legal order founded on the "hegemony" of the American and Western European tradition. This could be linked to a broader development philosophy that is founded on "balance of payment stability, a well managed fiscal budget, a market economy with a highly developed private business sector, and a reasonably developed capital market" (28).

5. Anthony Carty, ed., *Law and Development* (New York: New York University Press, 1992), xii. Carty suggests that this can be read as an apology for American development policy underlying the Foreign Assistance Legislation of 1966.

6. Franck, "New Development," 775.

7. Franck, "New Development," 771.

8. Franck, "New Development," 771.

9. Franck, "New Development," 771.

10. Franck, "New Development," 1969.

11. Paul Baran, *The Political Economy of Growth* (New York: Monthly Review Press, 1957), 142.

12. Ray Kiely, *Sociology and Development* (London: UCL Press, 1995), 40–47.

13. Immanuel Wallerstein, *The Modern World System* (New York: Academic Press, 1974).

14. Critics have tried to show that as dependency theory relied on Marxism, it was too clumsy to identify law's actual operation. Marxist thought tends to associate law with the superstructure rather than with the economic base. Law is seen as less central to social organization than it is to the economy. This is undoubtedly a poor reading of Marx, but the point here is to show that dependency theory offers much more than this reductivism.

15. Trubeck, *Towards a Social Theory of Law*, 150.

16. Trubeck, *Towards a Social Theory of Law*, 150.

17. Trubeck, *Towards a Social Theory of Law*, 151.

18. David F. Greenberg, "Law and Development in the Light of Dependency Theory," *Research in Law and Society* 3 (1980): 129–59.

19. Hideko Makiyama, *A New International Economic Order: Selected Documents Compiled*, Annex A, "I. International Development Policies Reviewed," United Nations Institute for Training and Research; New York (1982), report 320.

20. *UNCTAD Resolution on Review and Appraisal of the Implementation of the International Development Strategy, the Declaration and the Programme of Action on the Establishment of a New International Economic Order, the Charter of Economic Rights and Duties of States, and General Assembly Resolution on Development and International Economic Co-operation*, ed. Hideko Makiyama (New York: UNITAR, 1982), 320.

21. Annex A, "II. Appraisal of the Implementation of International Trade and Development Policies," report 320.

22. Subrata Roy Chowdhury, "Legal Status of the Charter of Economic Rights and Duties," in *Legal Aspects of the New International Economic Order*, ed. Kamal Hussein (London: Frances Pinter, 1980), 80.

23. Chowdhury, "Legal Status," 84.

24. Chowdhury, "Legal Status," 82–83.

25. Milan Bulajic, *Principles of International Development Law: Progressive Development of the Principles of International Law Relating to the New International Economic Order* (Dordrecht, Neth.: Martinus Nijhoff, 1986), 87.

26. Bulajic, *Principles*, 91.

27. These arguments are taken from Sarkar, *Development Law*. It is not suggested that they represent an adequate summary of the theoretical positions he develops; rather, they are offered as representative of a claim that development theory has moved beyond the impasse and finally found a new sense of its own maturity.

28. Sarkar, *Development Law*, 58.

29. Sarkar, *Development Law*, 59.

30. There are echoes of this doctrine in the most recent World Bank report that considers the doctrine of the rule of law. The World Bank has come to understand that the rule of law is central to development.

31. For instance, see Mohammed Bedjaoui, "Unorthodox Reflections on the Right to Development," in *International Law of Development: Comparative Perspectives*, ed. Francis Snyder and Peter Slinn (Abingdon, Eng.: Professional Books, 1987), 87–93. Bedjaoui attempts a more critical approach to the right to development. In the wake of the basic needs approach, the real issue is still the structural weakness of economies in less developed nations. So, how could a right to development be founded? Could a right to development find sure foundations on the notion of "solidarity" among nations? Bedjaoui asserts that "international solidarity" (96) is a fact resting on two interconnected issues: the interdependence of global economy and the "universal obligation" on states to develop the global economy. Bedjaoui's argument also relates to article 31 of the Charter of Economic Rights and Duties of States. He argues that the principle behind the article demands that developed nations have to give developing nations their "fair share," which "belongs by right." Bedjaoui also argues that "essential world food resources" are legally acknowledged as "the common heritage of mankind" (111). There are historical precedents for such a claim, contemporary with the very intellectual foundations of the notions of international law and community. Economically, Bedjaoui's argument is founded on Perroux's elaboration of "generalized reciprocity"; the theological underpinnings of this idea run through both Christian and Islamic cultures. In practical terms, this approach could be achieved by the foundation of a "universal institution" funded by a tax levied on "a few manufactured products of high added value" that are produced from materials originating in the Third World. The fund would act to "equalize" the distribution of food by buying surplus production from nations and offering it at a "token price" to those nations in need.

32. P. T. Muchlinski, "Basic Needs Theory and Development Law," in Snyder and Slinn, *International Law of Development*, 238.

111

33. Muchlinski, "Basic Needs Theory," 240.
34. Muchlinski, "Basic Needs Theory," 240.
35. Muchlinski, "Basic Needs Theory," 253.
36. Muchlinski, "Basic Needs Theory," 18.
37. Arturo Escobar, *Encountering Development: The Making and Unmaking of the Third World* (Princeton, N.J.: Princeton University Press, 1995), 292. See also, Vandana Shiva, *The Violence of the Green Revolution* (New Delhi: The Other India Press, 1991).
38. Escobar, *Encountering Development*, 300.
39. Escobar, *Encountering Development*, 194.
40. Escobar, *Encountering Development*, 196.
41. Escobar, *Encountering Development*, 195.
42. Escobar, *Encountering Development*, 293.
43. Escobar, *Encountering Development*, 195.
44. A key reference point is also the final document of the 1993 Vienna World Conference on Human Rights. Other sources would include the International Covenant on Economic, Social, and Cultural Rights (1966). In addition, references to the right to education and health care are found in the European Social Charter (1961), the African Charter on Human and Peoples' Rights (1981), and the Convention of the Rights of the Child (1989). Cited in Varun Gauri, *Social Rights and Economics Claims to Health Care and Education in Developing Countries* (Washington, D.C.: World Bank, 2003).
45. See Dani Brandt and Sage Russell, eds., *Exploring the Core Content of Socio-economic Rights* (Pretoria: Protea Book House, 2002).
46. World Bank, *Development and Human Rights: The Role of the World Bank*, at www-wds.worldbank.org/servlet/WDS_IBank_Servlet?pcont=details&eid =00 00 94946_01112004010066.
47. World Bank, *Implementation of Gender Mainstreaming Strategy: First Annual Monitoring Report*, 2003, at www-wds.worldbank.org/servlet/WDS_IBank _Servlet?pcont=details&eid=00 01 60016_20030519161831.
48. World Bank, *Implementation of Gender Mainstreaming Strategy*, 115.
49. World Bank, *Implementation of Gender Mainstreaming Strategy*, 16.
50. World Bank, *Implementation of Gender Mainstreaming Strategy*, 9.
51. Christian Aid, *Struggling to Be Heard: Democratising the World Bank and the IMF* (London: Christian Aid, 2003), 12.
52. *Struggling to Be Heard*, 8.
53. *Struggling to Be Heard*, 5.
54. *Struggling to Be Heard*, 6.
55. It draws on data made available by the Bank for International Settlements.
56. *Struggling to Be Heard*, 4.
57. *A Fair and Transparent Arbitration Process for Indebted Southern Coun-*

tries, at www.erlassjahr.de/15_publikationen/15_dokumente/englisch/ftap_en
glisch_rz.pdf. See also, the proposals for an *International Arbitration Mechanism on Debt* at www.afrodad.org/issues/18arbtration.htm.

58. *War on Want Report*, at www.waronwant.org/textonly/0143/www.war
onwant.org/?lid = 1443.

59. *War on Want Report*.

60. *War on Want Report*.

61. Escobar, *Encountering Development*, 220.

62. Henry J. Steiner and Philip Alston, *International Human Rights in Context* (Oxford: Oxford University Press, 2000), 1306.

WAR, RIGHTS, DEVELOPMENT, AND THE MARKET: THE RETREAT OF HUMANITY

> This war . . . is swiftly turning into a war for humanitarian principles.
>
> —Ben Macintyre, *Times* (London), April 4, 2003

> Bush, Blair, Saddam Hussein. The same. All liars.
>
> —Unnamed Iraqi woman

The Gulf War of 2003 and its aftermath bring together a complex conjunction of international law, human rights, and—particularly in the reconstruction of Iraq—the political economy of debt and trade. In this final chapter of the book, we will try to read these themes through the evocation of humanity made by the champions of human rights in the war against terrorism.[1] These final arguments range across a diverse field of legal and political materials. Once again, we should be careful. We are studying fragments: a field composed by its tensions and ideological struggles. It would be unwise to expect that a coherent jurisprudence of the global will emerge.

We will first examine the work of those scholars of international law who have made arguments about the legitimacy of military intervention. This body of scholarship utilizes diverse sources and claims to present human rights as the ethical or humanitarian foundation of international law. Although it is possible to credit the moral force of these arguments, they also occasion misgivings about the broader politics of their position. Interventions in the name of democracy and human

115

rights are made into the affairs of undeveloped Third World states or those nations who have lost the support of their Cold War backers. This political agenda makes the invasion of Israel in support of the human rights of Palestinians somewhat unlikely.

Many of these tensions return in the second part of the chapter, when we turn to review recent uses of force under the 1945 UN Charter. A use of force that draws on the UN Charter makes a claim to legitimization in terms of global humanity, human rights, and the struggle for international peace and security. As much as one might deplore the use of force, there are certain situations where force might be legitimate, where a failure to act could, for example, lead to genocide, as it did in Rwanda. However, we must be careful in pursuing these claims. Justifications for the war against terrorism add a new perspective to the old discourse on the use of force in international law. We must study closely the arguments that justify interventions in the invasions of Afghanistan, the first Iraq war, and the NATO action against Yugoslavia. These arguments will then be connected with different deployments of humanitarian law.

After the invasion of Iraq, the liberators are finding themselves in a complex position. They are bound by the Geneva and Hague conventions that relate to occupied territory. This form of humanitarian law must be formally distinguished from the form of humanitarian intervention outlined earlier, though the former is similar to the latter to the extent that each invokes humanity as its ground and justification. In postwar Iraq, the humanitarian obligations of the coalition forces have become bound up with the integration of the country into the global economy. In this area we encounter yet another inchoate area of jurisprudence, fraught with the tensions that exist between the humanitarian law and the prerogatives of the market.

The final section of this chapter returns to the justifications for the war and a certain ideology of human rights. How can the claims of the apologists for humanity, freedom, and the war against terror be weighed up? Where could we find the beginnings of a discourse that is equal to the traumas of our times?

The Jurisprudence of Intervention:
An Ethical International Law?

The Iraq War of 2003 prompts a reassessment of arguments in international law that have been used to justify military intervention in the past. Although not directly relevant to the political justifications for the war, these arguments are indicative of a broader set of tensions that relate to the legal structuring of relationships between developed and developing nations in international law and one important way in which the notion of humanitarianism has been given a specifically legal meaning.

Scholars of international law have been keen to develop a notion of humanitarianism that can be used to justify military intervention in the sovereign affairs of states that cannot guarantee the human rights of their citizens. A composite definition of this position can be hazarded: a state may use force or exert control over the internal affairs of another state to the extent that such actions are justifiable with reference to basic human rights or the laws of humanity.[2] Lying behind this claim is a coordination of law with the interests of humanity, as represented by a nation acting on behalf of human rights. Apologists of this view have stressed that justifications of intervention are as old as the Westphalian system. Intervention arguments developed around the great European religious wars and took a recognizably contemporary form toward the end of the nineteenth century. This is reflected within the textbook tradition. The editor of *Oppenheim's International Law* asserts that although a state has sovereign discretion over the treatment of its subjects, "intervention in the interests of humanity is legally permissible."[3] Other scholars have pointed out that although there is no clear consensus of the precise terms of the doctrine within customary international law, there are "consistent views" held on the subject matter.[4] Where does this leave us?

Even if the right to intervention may not have clear legal authority, it may be that an argument could be made about the coherence of intervention within the wider interests of humanity. Of late, scholars and commentators have found this approach particularly compelling. We could link it to a certain rethinking of the doctrine of sovereignty or, rather, the sovereignty of those nations who, from an international perspective, are seen as incapable of upholding the human rights of their citizens. Perez de Cuellar is cited by one scholar as observing that the post–Second World War situation is marked by "an irresistible shift in public attitude towards the belief that the defense of the oppressed in the name of morality should prevail over frontiers and legal documents."[5] This is part of a wider discourse where, to be precise, sovereignty is not rejected but linked to the claim that a government is only legitimate to the extent that it can protect the rights of those on whom it calls for allegiance. A government's duty to protect the rights of its citizens would prevent the systematic oppression of ethnic minorities and encourage effective response to humanitarian crises brought about by either natural disaster or civil war. To justify intervention by a foreign state in the latter situation, a national government must be unable to mobilize the resources to protect refugees or guarantee the safety of large numbers of people. Of course, the issue we are addressing here tends to be associated less with famine relief or help in the face of natural disaster and more with a right for nations to intervene in the affairs of a sovereign state to end civil war or prevent the collapse of state structures.[6]

One of the most celebrated developments of the interventionist argument in relation to sovereign states points toward the realization of an ethical international law.[7] This approach begins with the notion that morality, in a primary sense, describes the acts of individuals. Starting with the individual means that one cannot properly talk of the rights of states. Governments are thus mere "agents" of their people, deriving their mandate to govern from the individuals who make up the state.[8] Intervention is justifiable to the extent that it seeks to bring to an end human rights violations. One needs to therefore distinguish between just and unjust intervention. "Collateral nonhumanitarian motives"— the need to build regional alliances, for example—should be limited to the extent that they are compatible with the primary objective of protecting human rights. The test to determine legitimate intervention also stresses that it is not justifiable to infringe human rights as a means of protecting the human rights of the "target" state.[9] This is bolstered by the principle of "proportionality"—that is, any intervention must be proportional to the possibility of bringing an end to the human rights abuses that have occasioned intervention.[10] Finally, the "victims of oppression must welcome the intervention."[11] This theory is clearly driven by its sense of ethical duty and an impatience with the moral evasions that come from legal positivism, a theory "blind to the moral dimensions of politics."[12]

A slightly different articulation of this "right" sees it as developing from the entitlement to self-determination. The right takes a concrete form in the "normative entitlement" to participate in free and fair elections, a right that can be policed through the international monitoring of elections.[13] Significant reform would be necessary before this right becomes realized in international practice. However, if reforms could be achieved, then governments legitimized by fair elections would qualify for protection from intervention.[14] Others have suggested that there are positive sources for this right. One could have regard to the International Covenant on Civil and Political Rights (1976), in particular article 25. Other sources would include the first protocol to the European Convention on Human Rights, the American Convention on Human Rights, and, in a more limited sense, the African Charter on Human and Peoples' Rights. Further support can be drawn from UN election monitors' reports. If one were to abstract from these documents, one would be able to formulate a composite right having four "elements": "universal and equal suffrage"; the necessity for "a secret ballot"; the requirement that elections take place within a reasonable time frame; and a prohibition on discrimination against voters or the parties themselves.[15]

There are certainly problems with any articulation of this right, not least the "inconsistency" with which nondemocratic regimes have been treated.[16] The litigation over the right of Gibraltarians to vote in elections for the Parliament of the European Union also suggests a plethora of difficulties.[17] Furthermore, from the perspective of the UN Charter, such arguments are unacceptable. Although it is accurate to say that the notion of sovereignty has been qualified, this does not allow one to assert that the promotion of democracy, rather than the preservation of peace, has become the founding principle of the UN. We must now turn to look at the UN Charter in more depth.

The United Nations, International Law, and the Use of Force

Whether or not a right to intervention exists in customary law or in the customs of nations, some would argue that the UN Charter states the law correctly. If nations do not adhere to the charter, negative consequences would follow in international relations. We need to look at the development of this doctrine and the strains to which it has been subjected in the last decade. We will briefly review the law of the charter and then turn to see how the law has developed.

First, consider the text of article 2.4:

All Members shall refrain in their international relations from the threat or use of force against the territorial integrity or political independence of any state, or in any other manner inconsistent with the Purposes of the United Nations.

Article 2 of the UN Charter places an absolute prohibition on the use or threat of force against a state in its territorial and political manifestations, with two exceptions. The UN Security Council can authorize the use of force with reference to chapter 7. Chapter 7 covers actions that can be taken with regard to "threats to the peace, breaches of the peace and acts of aggression." The only other exception to the prohibition on the use of force is the right to self-defense under article 51. This is an "inherent right" belonging to individual or collective action in the event of "armed attack." However, recourse to action does not detract from the "authority and responsibility of the Security Council" to take whatever action is necessary to "maintain or restore" peace.

So, how has intervention been justified under the UN charter? Article 24.1 places the "primary responsibility for the maintenance of international peace and security" on the Security Council. If 24.1 is read alongside article 39, then the Security Council can make use of its powers under chapter 7 on occasions where there is a "threat to the peace, breach of the peace, or act of aggression." Under chapter 7, the Security Council can take a number of courses of action. These range from calling on the parties concerned to comply with measures that the Security Council considers necessary (article 39); deciding the measures to be employed, short of the use of armed force (article 41); and taking such action as is necessary to "maintain or restore international peace and security" (article 42).

As the role of the UN has changed significantly with the end of the Cold War, the use of the powers outlined here can be analyzed as falling into two different periods. Before 1990, there were only two instances in which the Security Council had ordered "enforcement actions." These occasions reflected the politics of the Cold War. As it was possible for UN action to be prevented by a veto from one of the permanent members of the Security Council, the political differences and the power blocs existing between nations meant that UN action was easily thwarted. The response of the UN was to promulgate the "Uniting for Peace" resolution, which provided that in the face of a veto, the assembly would make recommendations that could include force. In 1950, the Security Council recommended that members of the UN furnish "such assistance" as "may be necessary" to help the Republic of Korea repel armed attack, an operation under the command of the United States. China's intervention in Korea was condemned under the Uniting for Peace doctrine. Later, in 1966, the British government was called on by a resolution of the council to prevent the breach of sanctions against Southern Rhodesia, using force if necessary. Slightly earlier (1960–1964), the use of force "if necessary" was authorized in the case of peacekeeping operations in the Congo. Sanctions were also imposed upon Southern Rhodesia (1966–1979) and South Africa (1977–1994).[18]

With the end of the Cold War, the UN played a "far more active role."[19] Wider interpretations were given to the notion of a "threat to peace" under article 39. In the changed political circumstances, the UN became more interventionist. However, the case of Somalia (1992–1993) is central. The case of Somalia is somewhat different from the other cases considered here as it shows how chapter 7 could be invoked when a "humanitarian crisis" occurred as a result of internal conflict or civil war. Resolution 733 (1992) thus addresses the concern that the loss of life, the material destruction, and the "consequences for the stability and peace in the region" were a threat to international security. A later resolution (746) was even more precise in its concern for the humanitarian crisis. Further deteriorations in the situation in Somalia and the inability of the UN to deliver aid led to the council's authorizing military intervention by the United States to establish a "secure environment for humanitarian relief operations."[20] The setbacks suffered by U.S. forces led to the withdrawal of the expeditionary force and a volteface in the terms of the UN operation.

Perhaps the problems experienced in Somalia were one reason why the UN did not respond effectively in Rwanda. In the face of massacres of the minority Tutsi by the majority Hutus, the UN appeared to do nothing. In 1994, it passed resolution 918 acknowledging that the "magnitude of the killings" constituted a threat to international peace and security and that there was a need for humanitarian intervention. However, the United States was reluctant to commit troops, as it did not consider that its interests were under threat or that there was a clear set of objectives for action. Western European powers also refrained from intervention, and most official discourses on Rwanda avoided the word *genocide* for fear that acknowledging the scale of the killings would compel action. Some African nations showed that they were willing to contribute to a UN mission, but military action under French leadership was not authorized until some months later, in resolution 929. Critics have questioned the motivation of Operation Turquoise, suggesting that French intervention was to prop up the government of General Habyarimana's Hutu regime.[21] Rwanda thus represents the failure of humanitarian intervention. Had there been a will to act, Western states would have "secured a Chapter VII mandate. . . . It is inconceivable that the Security Council would have blocked this."[22]

In moving from the case of Rwanda to the issue of Iraq and Afghanistan, it may become clear that intervention in the name of human rights is forthcoming only when it is linked to certain military objectives and interests. The war against terrorism redefines the entire field.

Failed States and the War against Terrorism:
From Kosovo to Iraq

The UN resolutions enabling actions against the Iraqi invasion of Kuwait opened a new phase in the development of the doctrines that we have been examining. Of late, British prime minister Tony Blair has referred to the justification of the Iraq war in terms of human rights and humanitarianism rather than simply a search for weapons of mass destruction.[23] It may be possible, in jurisprudential terms to bring together human rights and humanitarianism as the real grounds of an argument justifying the invasion of Iraq.

We need to review the development of a jurisprudence that relates to military intervention in the Gulf, although this means that we have to briefly engage with NATO actions against Serbia in 1999.

Resolution 678 (1990) authorized member states "to use all necessary force" in cooperation with the government of Kuwait "to restore international peace and security in the area." As Bowring writes, this was the first time since 1950 (when resolution 84 authorized military action against North Korea) that unified military action was taken with the "approval of the Security Council."[24] It would be hasty, though, to see this resolution as unproblematically providing support for humanitarian intervention. Some commentators saw it as a measure promoting collective self-defense.[25] Others saw it as illegitimate, as it departed from the charter's stress on nonviolence. The exceptional degree of international pressure that made the resolution possible also suggests that it is unreliable as a precedent; likewise, resolution 688 (1991), concerning the Kurds in the north of Iraq, has been criticized as a "dubious precedent."[26] The resolution did not refer to chapter 7, and the reference to internal conflict was limited to the negative effects of transborder incursions and the flow of refugees.

We need to take a few steps back to understand other arguments used to justify the invasion of Iraq, and we need to look to resolution 713 (1991), adopted as a response to the tensions that were attendant on the breakup of Yugoslavia. Fighting was "a threat to international peace and security." Commentators suggest that resolution 714 could be seen as the UN's affirming its right to intervene by imposing an arms embargo. This does not necessarily mean, though, that the UN was making a general assertion of a right to intervene to prevent a threat to the peace. The Security Council passed resolution 770 in 1992. It made reference to chapter 7. Member states were empowered to use "all measures necessary" to aid in the delivery of "humanitarian assistance." Those resolutions did not have the desired affect as the relief convoys had inadequate military protection. A further resolution, 781, backed up by resolution 816, created "no fly zones" enforced by NATO planes. Those measures did not resolve the increasing ethnic tensions. Attempts by the UN to condemn both sides and to support a greater measure of autonomy for Albanians in Kosovar also failed to achieve stability in the region. Finally, in 1998, resolution 1199 was passed. The UN ordered a cease-fire so that the humanitarian situation could be improved. The resolution stated that if these and other demands made on the Federal Republic of Yugoslavia were not accepted, it would be necessary to "consider further action."[27]

It would appear that the NATO decision to act was not authorized by this resolution nor by a later one, resolution 1203, which did not contain a reference to the use of force. However, in the view of the United States, action was legitimized to avoid wider destabilization and avert the humanitarian crisis. Prime Minister Blair also justified the action with reference to both the need to protect Albanian citizens in Kosovar and the broader moral imperative for action.[28] Other arguments made by U.K. officials stressed that the action was a legal response to an exceptional situation and a deepening humanitarian crisis. As Bowring points out, international lawyers were divided as to whether, in the light of the bombing of Serbia, customary international law had developed a right to avert humanitarian disaster through state practice and *opinio juris* that trumped the UN charter. The Independent Commission on Kosovo found that NATO actions were illegal but legitimate. This could be countered with the objection that this defense of humanitarian intervention is merely a new form of imperialism. The sovereignty of small countries can be suspended when it does not accord with the views of the hegemonic powers. Kosovo subverted the charter by showing that the United Kingdom and the United States develop international law to suit their interests.

This trend continued as a response to September 11, 2001. It has been noted that the UN resolutions following the atrocity (1368 and 1373) stressed the right of self-defense.[29] Indeed, the U.S. defense of its action was based on self-defense.[30] Although Kofi Annan's statement "reaffirmed" the right of nations to act in self-defense, it should not be read as an endorsement of the invasion of Afghanistan. It was a notification that military action was under way.[31] A somewhat different interpretation of events sees in resolution 1373 the implicit acknowledgment that force could be used.[32] Making reference to chapter 7, the resolution is framed in terms of the United Nation's decision that states "take the necessary steps to prevent the commission of terrorist actions." The necessary steps could include military intervention. However, it would seem a somewhat strained interpretation of this resolution to argue that it redefines the charter's focus on nonintervention and nonviolence. The debate continues. One commentator argues that that the right to self-defense is entirely separate from the charter. Unilateralism is affirmed by arguing that a state has a right to self-defense.[33] As Bowring comments, it appears that "the Security Council, and in effect, the whole of the Charter and customary law on the use of force and self-defense, have been jettisoned in the name of the war against terrorism."[34]

The most recent invasion of Iraq also makes use of a chapter 7 argument. Although there is presently a certain degree of obfuscation involved in arguments justifying war, we can offer some provisional comments. From the perspective of the British government, the authority to make use of force against Iraq is contained in a series of UN resolutions that have to be read together. It is an argument that returns to chapter 7 of the charter. The earliest resolution in the series is 678, which authorizes the uses of force to end the Iraqi invasion of Kuwait and restore international peace and security. In a later resolution, 687, conditions were imposed after the cease-fire to ensure that Iraq "eliminated" its weapons of mass destruction. This resolution "suspended" but did not "terminate" the authority to use force in the event of noncompliance. It could thus be argued that a "material breach" of 687 authorizes the use of force. This can be conjoined with an argument made with reference to resolution 1441. In that resolution, the Security Council states that Iraq was in material breach, as it had failed to comply with the obligations imposed by resolution 687. The threat of "serious consequences" contained in 1441 effectively authorizes the use of force that had, until that point, remained suspended. The argument also affirms that it was not necessary for an explicit authorization of force by the Security Council; rather, a report to the council on Iraq's continuing breach would prove sufficient trigger.[35]

There are many problems attendant on this jurisprudence of the war. Moreover, one has the sense that arguments are shifting. The weapons of mass destruction justification is being generalized so that interventionist arguments are coming closer to those that use human rights as a ground for military action.[36] To some extent, however, this issue has become superseded by the problems faced by the occupying forces. It is as if any inchoate jurisprudence on military intervention would also have to consider the duties placed on occupying powers by international law, duties that bring together humanitarianism with arguments about the international market.[37]

The Jurisprudence of Reconstruction: Humanity and the Open Market

If a nation resorts to war, victory brings with it certain legal obligations. We must turn to a different source of humanitarian law and look at the way law structures the military and civil reconstruction of occupied territory. We will see that the Hague Convention places particular obligations on the occupying power; but this position must, in turn, be understood with reference to the ongoing attempts to rebuild Iraq. This reconstruction sees the humanitarian law of war coming into contact with the laws of the market and international capital.

Section 3 of the Hague Convention applies to military authority exercised over an occupied state. This convention presently applies to Iraq, as it is under the authority of the coalition forces (article 42). It is useful to quickly overview the key provisions. The convention is realistic, as it recognizes that the authority of occupying forces can only extend to those areas that are effectively under their control. Article 43 places a duty on the coalition to restore public order while respecting local (Iraqi) law. There is also a duty to respect "family honor," persons lives, and private property. This extends to religious convictions. The obligations of the convention also refer to the ongoing tasks of government. Continuing the taxation policies and practices of the previous government can finance the administration of occupied territory. There is a provision that allows for an extra levy to cover military expenses, but there is also a prohibition in article 50 against punitive taxation. Furthermore, any requisitions demanded by occupying forces must be proportionate to the resources of the occupied country. The occupying power is to administrate the property that belonged to the previous government, and the capital of those properties must be preserved. Property belonging to religious and cultural institutions, even if belonging to the state, is treated under the convention as private property.

The convention draws a distinction between the way in which the occupying power treats the property of citizens and the property of the former government. A clear line must be drawn between the power of appropriation and the earlier duty (article 46) that forbids the confiscation of private property. In general, citizens cannot be made to swear allegiance to the occupying power or contribute to its military operations, but occupying forces can confiscate government and military property and resources. Article 53 allows the occupying forces to take possession of "cash, funds, and realizable securities" that were "strictly the property of the State." The convention allows occupying forces to take over all "depots of arms, means of transport, stores and supplies" that can be used for military purposes. This power extends to the confiscation of telecommunication and transport systems. If these assets belong to private citizens, though, ownership must be restored at the end of hostilities, with compensation paid.

While the Hague Convention may determine the legal regime that

applies to the occupied territory, in the reconstruction of Iraq, human-
istic and business concerns intermingle.[38] The reconstruction of Iraq
sees the conjunction of many of the themes that we have been studying
throughout this book. In the words of the World Bank and the UN,
Iraq must be transformed from a centralized, state-run bureaucracy to
a market economy.

There can be no argument about the scale of the task. Not only must
the country be repaired after the devastation of the last two wars, but
the deep-seated economic stagnation and social dislocation must be
confronted. Economic infrastructures such as roads, pipelines, and
communications systems have degraded. The Baathist command economy was corrupt and overly centralized. Dominant in all sectors, it was
committed to its own perpetuation, rather than to the objectives of
sound management and sustained growth. Furthermore, sanctions imposed against the country "isolated" it from "global trends," resulting in
"fossilized structures of production and commerce."[39]

One might think that there is a strange privileging of information in
these discourses on the Iraqi economy, where the damage wrought by
the old regime is described, but the destruction wrought by the war of
liberation is glossed over. However, we do not have the space here to
look in detail at the constitution of the discourse on reconstruction. We
need to overview some key themes. Our primary concern is with the
legal and economic constitution of the reconstruction. This is inher-
ently cooperative. Increasingly, the United States is finding that reconstruction demands cooperation between itself and other nations. U.S.
Treasury secretary John Snow, in an address to the G7 finance minis-
ters, stressed this very theme: cooperation between nations and the
need to coordinate with the IMF and the World Bank. The "donor's
fund," set up in the aftermath of the Afghanistan war, was invoked as a
precedent. The task of governing a nation as large and ethnically diverse as Iraq may mean that it is beyond the resources of any one nation. The meeting of the Donor Conference in October 2003 brought
together various parties who were concerned with the reconstruction of
the country: the United Arab Emirates, the United States, the European
Union, and Japan, assisted by the UN Development Group, the World
Bank Group, and the IMF. That the United Nations Development Program is also actively involved is not just a reflection of its long-term

involvement in Iraq but suggests that the development mission is now thoroughly integrated into postconflict reconstruction. Indeed, the scale of the reconstruction shows how humanitarian, military, and economic objectives are combined.[40]

Iraq is not just war-ravaged; it is significantly in debt. However, it may be that Iraq's debts will be treated differently from the other debt problems that we have examined. There may be aid in repaying loans to the World Bank affected by European powers and Japan. The precise forms of cooperation would depend on the demands made by the nation's creditors. At present, Iraq's creditors are the IMF, the World Bank, various governments that had provided trade credits and bilateral loans, and private banks and companies. The structure of Iraqi debt is such that only $1.1 billion is owed to "the first group." If those creditors can be reassured, then the involvement of other actors would depend entirely on the reconstruction package. There are two options: a package modeled on the Marshall Plan, which rebuilt Europe from 1945 onward, or one orientated to private finance.[41] The dynamics of the situation are such that there is a need to involve both economic and humanitarian aspects of reconstruction in whatever plan is finally determined.

The reconstruction of Iraq is largely predicated on creating a viable form of capitalism. The international community is moving on two fronts. First, there has to be a resolution of the security situation, the repair and updating of utilities, the encouragement of private investment, and the renewed production of oil. Iraq must then be repositioned in the world economy. IMF/World Bank policy, announced in Dubai, favors market-based reforms that will affect all areas of the economy. The United States is currently making transfers to the Central Bank of Iraq to increase its international reserves, and there will have to be significant reforms in the domestic banking system to open the country up to foreign investment. Private finance will prove essential in the rebuilding of the economy because "public resources are unlikely to adequately provide the needed volume of investment."[42] Indeed, the ultimate aim would be for Iraq to seek entry into the WTO.[43] In the short term, however, the WTO has argued that the most immediate aims for the trade regime would be to raise revenues through effective taxation. Acknowledging the demands of the situation, the WTO is willing to allow exemptions from a low-tariff regime, but any high tariffs would have to be carefully controlled and eventually reduced.

Oil remains the key to recovery. However, it seems to be suggested by the World Bank/UN report that international assistance will only be sufficient to rebuild basic institutions. Any necessary investment to further increase in productivity will have to be from private sources. It is also necessary to raise a "reconstruction levy" on imported goods and to put in place a system of taxation that would be levied on what domestic production remains. State-owned enterprises would have to be either shut down or restructured. So, to speak of Iraq as a "transitional economy" is to speak of a special case. Economic repositioning has to make use of oil, but profound problems remain.

Policy is not restricted to these macroeconomic considerations. The discourse on governance also goes into action in Iraq, demanding transparent and accountable institutions. A much broader discourse on the role of "stakeholders" in Iraqi economy and society has also been initiated. Reconstruction cannot only be driven in a top-down fashion but must be encouraged and nurtured by civil society, nongovernmental organizations, and ongoing institutional reform. The focus is on building "viable local institutions."[44] Although reinvigorating local institutions is a necessary counter to the years of centralized authoritarian government, there must be a linking of locality and center in the delivery of resources. There is thus a role for community-based organizations that will manage resources and coordinate efforts to develop the health and education sectors, microfinance initiatives, and local councils and civic organizations.

The UN and the World Bank's governance agenda is also evident in the provision of rule-of-law reforms throughout Iraq "providing services in human rights, judicial training, legal assistance and support for independent media."[45] UN discourses on development are framed in terms of "cross-cutting themes": human rights, gender, and environmentalism. We will consider the first two. The dictatorship had led to large-scale human rights abuses and to the inability of the judiciary to preserve the rule of law. It is necessary to make sure that the independence of the judiciary is guaranteed, that a human rights culture is "institutionalized," and that the exclusion of certain groups is redressed. Central to the restructuring of civil society is the inculcation of a human rights culture.[46] Gender considerations are also apparent. Official policy in 1990 had led to restrictions on movement for women and decreased employment opportunities. As a great many households are headed by single women there is a clear need for mainstreaming policies and for addressing inequalities in earnings and social position. These concerns tend to be bracketed together and presented as the need for a fundamental reinvigoration of democratic culture, with the formal institutions to match. The approach of these international institutions, then, is to see economic and political reform as inseparable.

Alongside this discourse on governance, rights, and participation is the opening of Iraq to private companies and investors. The reconstruction of Iraq is particularly attractive, offering many more opportunities than those that existed in the aftermath of the 1991 Gulf War. The country's oil revenues and the return of skilled Iraqis from exile abroad make for enticing construction and development prospects. The key issue is whether the ability to award contracts will rest with the United States as the de facto power or with the UN as the administrator of the country.[47]

If the United States retained this power to award contracts, then the consensus appears to be that it will be used as a way of rewarding friends and allies. For instance, it is thought that Fiat will benefit, as will the Spanish construction company Fomentos de Construcciones y Contratas. The French company TotalFinaElf is predicted to be one loser, as it had a contract with the Iraqi government for future rights over certain oil fields. The contract would have gone into effect once sanctions were lifted. Litigation may be forthcoming, as is the likelihood that the Turks will be rewarded for remaining out of the war and refraining from invading Kurdish-controlled territories. Construction contracts will thus be awarded to Turkish companies. This is alongside the congressional vote of $1 billion in "economic assistance" to Turkey. The contracts for the reconstruction of Iraq are estimated at $100 billion.[48] European companies were placing pressure on their governments to make their cases to the American administration, and the *International Herald Tribune* reported a "corporate scramble" that extended to "corporate scouts" operating with military forces in Iraq. Corporate scouts are "reserve officers" who, while fulfilling military functions, identify business opportunities.[49]

What sense can we make of this?

Humanitarian Intervention and the Disappearance of Humanity: The Naked Lunch of the Law

How can we account for the distortions and deployments of "humanity," this concept that should be coordinate with our understanding of the global?

In the final lines of this chapter, I suggest that our concern has always been with a particular knotting of concepts, a conjunction of themes that is capable of producing an understanding of law and globalization, of illuminating certain processes. Throughout this book, we have repeatedly seen that the law makes sense to the extent that one is able to grasp its embeddedness in various contexts. But this is not to say that law can only be understood with reference to its context. Law clearly has its own specificity, its own organization, even though the theme of at least one of the chapters is the extent to which this organization is now involved with processes that are economic or policy driven. In this chapter we have also seen that it is not possible to achieve a coherent overview of the legal principles that are playing themselves out in this area. The ultimate conjunction, where the law of military intervention encounters the laws and demands of the market, is the most fraught. Perhaps at this very moment, with this very equation, law's naked lunch becomes apparent; we can see what is on the end of the juristic fork, and it is not a pretty sight.

Rather than read the economic overdetermination of the law as the "superiority" of international capital to any noble or naïve claims about human rights, it is preferable to see such overdetermination, at least for the moment, as the site of a particular disappearance. It is the moment at which one of the supposed aims of war, humanitarian intervention, disappears; or, the speed of its disappearance accelerates. We will solicit the help of a concept, if this is indeed what it is, drawn from an ongoing work that travels under a variety of names but one that we can understand as an ongoing study of the constitution of the political as a global phenomenon.[50]

How can the idea of politics as a retreat help us to consider law's situation? We need to return to the problem introduced in the paragraph that opens this concluding section of the chapter. The philosophical or general account is not outside the processes it observes; rather, it occupies a "reciprocal" relationship. It is no more prior to the law or

131

to politics than these terms are independent of the philosophical. This reciprocal constitution of different discourses attests to our own situation or "state"; our intellectual engagement with any given moment is in part determined by an inheritance, a set of concepts and ways of thinking. To refer back to the notion of the reciprocal, this "moment" is the coming together of different instances to define a problematic. That these ideas come from classical roots is not difficult to show, but we do need to be clear about historical development.[51]

The very notion of human rights, or humanity realized in the law, is predicated on an inheritance that can be traced back to Roman and Greek ideas that were received and developed in Christian and post-Christian Europe. But to be more precise, we are concerned with a far more recent instantiation of this history that can be dated from the conclusion of the Second World War. This is the ongoing opposition of human rights to something identified as totalitarianism. We have seen that the postwar settlement, bringing together economy and human rights, does so in the defeat of two perceived totalitarianisms: those of Nazi Germany and Soviet Communism. The belated "defeat" of the latter is linked to the (supposed) hegemonic rise of a world order that can now speak for a triumphant humanity. Humanity appears to find its destiny, its global realization, in a particular epoch of human rights.[52]

Let us see how these reflections might apply to one text that celebrates this appearance and this coming of age. Of course, this is not to suggest that the following passage should be taken as defining its field. There are other versions of human rights and the international community. We are interested in this passage because it articulates an extreme—an influential extreme:

> The great struggles of the twentieth century between liberty and totalitarianism ended with a decisive victory for the forces of freedom—and a single sustainable model for national success: freedom, democracy, and free enterprise. In the twenty-first century, only nations that share a commitment to protecting basic human rights and guaranteeing political and economic freedom will be able to unleash the potential of their people and assure their future prosperity. People everywhere want to be able to speak freely; choose who will govern them; worship as they please; educate their children—male and female; own property; and enjoy the benefits of their labor. These values of freedom are right and

true for every person, in every society—and the duty of protecting these values against their enemies is the common calling of freedom-loving people across the globe and across the ages.

As we defend the peace, we will also take advantage of an historic opportunity to preserve the peace. . . . America will encourage the advancement of democracy and economic openness in both nations, because these are the best foundations for domestic stability and international order. We will strongly resist aggression from other great powers—even as we welcome their peaceful pursuit of prosperity, trade, and cultural advancement.[53]

We need to read these texts at a number of different levels and in a number of different registers. There is, of course, a measure of rhetoric to these passages, and we should be aware that we are reading a form of victory oration. One of the main organizing tropes, which is indeed part of both a rhetoric and a substance, is the notion of teleology. We have arrived. Rights are located in a historical narrative, a narrative with which we are familiar. But this narrative moves toward the gate of the "now." We have choices that no others have had to face. These choices summon us into the presence of certain historical themes, but it is only now that we can appreciate the logic of history and the pattern that lies within. The great struggles have concluded in the victory of freedom—a freedom that has a very specific constitution and value. There is now only one form of economic organization that can allow for the equation of human rights and prosperity.

Note how the economics of free enterprise are associated unproblematically with a discourse of human rights: a catalogue that binds a set of rights that run freedom of conscience with a freedom to hold property. It is thus impossible to lose sight here of a particular form of Christianity, or a history that expresses itself as a movement from theological domination to a realization of the necessity and correct positioning of religion in a social structure. That these "freedoms are right and true" has two consequences. They are true for all peoples at all times; those that deny them must be denounced as enemies.

There are further tropes here worthy of our attention. In some ways this is the most troubling and profound statement of the global community. It appears to be on a specific set of terms. The cost of inclusion into community is economic, legal, and theological. It is based on a philosophical ground, the ability to posit the common substance, the human essence. The passage is ultimately a statement of political philosophy. It makes for a claim of right: a juristic or legal claim. Community includes members into itself and, at this very same moment, determines its enemy. But this enemy is involved in a war that is described as the preservation of the peace. The peace, as the most desired human state, then, is to be associated with the global, inclusive, cosmopolitan community. Peace lies within the walls of its city. Outside are the pagans, the barbarians, and the mad mullahs. History is completed by this announcement of the empire of law.

Something is clearly in retreat; something has been abandoned in this triumphalism about the global space and human rights. Perhaps something withdraws in this very act of positing its essence. Let us return to the anonymous quotation that opens this chapter: "Bush, Blair, Saddam Hussein. The same. All liars."

An unnamed speaker, unaccredited words; a woman interviewed in the ruins of Basra. The violence committed to her and to her words, the demand for a response, a sound bite for Western media, for the folks back home, is not lessened by the use of these words in the present context. But as this statement has entered the archive of the war, we should try to read its strangeness. It is strange from at least two perspectives: the statement reflects a certain disenchantment with her liberators but also with the man who was meant to speak for her, the president who was meant to be the embodiment of the nation. We could perhaps try to re-create its context to make sense of this double refusal. Explicit is a denial of sovereignties, whether that of humanitarian intervention or that of the regime from which she is meant to have been liberated. Moreover, there appears to be an explicit claim to the truth, but perhaps this is the greatest misreading. Perhaps this woman is done with the truth or with those that would articulate truths for her. In this negation, there is perhaps the retreat of humanity. At the same time, as humanity in its warring forms, as represented by the leaders of the free and the enslaved, becomes absent, there is the space of a refusal that is also the point, the time of reinvention. At the risk of committing yet another violence to these words, that of intellectualizing despair, perhaps, if there is hope—if the global can be decently spoken at all—it is, for the moment, this refusal.

—Santa Cruz De Tenerife 2003

Notes

1. Some essential texts that help in developing a perspective on this fraught term are as follows: Mark B. Salter, *Barbarians and Civilization in International Relations* (London: Pluto, 2002); John Cooley, *Unholy Wars* (London: Pluto, 2002); and David Chandler, *From Kosovo to Kabul: Human Rights and International Intervention* (London: Pluto, 2002). On legal responses, see John Strawson, ed., *Law after Ground Zero* (London: Glasshouse, 2002).

2. This combines aspects of Abiew's definition—see Francis Kofi Abiew, *The Evolution of the Doctrine and Practice of Humanitarian Intervention* (The Hague: Kluwer Law International, 1999)—with that of Ellery Stowell in *Intervention in International Law* (Washington, D.C.: John Byrne, 1921) and Fernando R. Teson, *Humanitarian Intervention: An Inquiry into Law and Morality* (Dobbs Ferry, N.Y.: Transnational Publishers, 1988), 5.

3. Sir Harrt Lauterpacht, ed., *Oppenheim's International Law* (London: Longmans, 1905), 347.

4. Abiew, *Evolution*, 43.

5. Abiew, *Evolution*, 223.

6. Abiew, *Evolution*, 250–51. The NGO community's response to military intervention is ambivalent. Some have argued that the more active response of the Security Council to intervene in the name of peace and security has been of assistance; others, such as Save the Children, have suggested, with reference to Somalia, that military intervention tends to cause more problems than it solves. See Save the Children, *African Rights, Humanitarianism Unbound: Current Dilemmas Facing Multi Mandate Relief Operations in Political Emergencies* (London: November 1994). Attention has also been drawn, though, to the willingness of national governments to put aid agencies in difficult and dangerous situations without sufficient resources for their protection. Commentators have argued that it is precisely this problem that would legitimize UN military protection as an integral aspect of some relief operations. The experience of certain agencies in the former Yugoslavia is given as evidence to support this position; Medecins sans Frontiers has changed its opposition to military intervention in the light of the genocide in Rwanda; the International Commission of the Red Cross has suggested that military deployments could have prevented deaths; and Oxfam has argued that the Rwandan tragedy should lead to a review of the position developed in Somalia.

7. Teson, *Humanitarian Intervention*, 116.

8. Teson, *Humanitarian Intervention*, 117.

9. Teson, *Humanitarian Intervention*, 21.

10. Teson, *Humanitarian Intervention*, 122.

11. Teson, *Humanitarian Intervention*, 126.

12. Teson, *Humanitarian Intervention*, 129.

13. It is admitted, though, that the present system is far from perfect.

14. Thomas M. Franck, "The Emerging Right to Democratic Governance," *American Journal of International Law* 86, no. 46 (1992): 47–91, quote at 91.

15. Gregory H. Fox, "The Right to Political Participation in International Law," in *Democratic Governance and International Law*, ed. Gregory H. Fox and Brad R. Roth (Cambridge: Cambridge University Press, 2000), 48–90, quote at 69.

16. James Crawford, "Democracy and the Body of International Law," in Fox and Roth, *Democratic Governance*, 91–120, quote at 117.

17. *Matthews v. UK*, application number 24833/94, February 18, 1999.

18. The doctrine of peacekeeping that was current in the Cold War also built on the Uniting for Peace recommendation. Article 11.2 was used as the formal mechanisms that enabled the General Assembly to recommend an operation if so requested by a state or with the consent of that state. Military force, however, fell under the jurisdiction of the Security Council. This was one of the factors feeding into the development of peacekeeping missions that were not active uses of force but were limited to observation and founded on "principles of consent." However, up to 1989, the majority of peacekeeping operations were Security Council authorized.

19. Figures are indicative. During the first forty-four years of the UN's operation, twenty-four Security Council resolutions made reference to chapter 7. "By 1993, it was adopting that many such resolutions each year" (Simon Chesterman, *Just War or Just Peace? Humanitarian Intervention and International Law* [Oxford: Oxford University Press, 2001], 121). Peacekeeping operations with authorization by the Security Council numbered thirty-five by the end of 1999.

20. Chesterman, *Just War or Just Peace*, 142.

21. Nicholas J. Wheeler, *Saving Strangers: Humanitarian Intervention in International Society* (Oxford: Oxford University Press, 2000), 234.

22. Wheeler, *Saving Strangers*, 241.

23. *The Independent*, September 26, 2003.

24. Bill Bowring, "The Degradation of International Law," in *Law after Ground Zero*, ed. John Strawson (Portland, Ore.: Glasshouse Press, 2002), 8.

25. Bill Bowring, "Degradation," 8 (quoting Rostow).

26. Chesterman, *Just War or Just Peace?* 131.

27. Chesterman, *Just War or Just Peace?* 209.

28. Chesterman, *Just War or Just Peace?* 211. See also, BBC reports of April 3, 1999, at http://news.bbc.co.uk/1/hi/uk_politics/326763.stm. Prime Minister Blair insisted that the action against Serbia was a "just cause." There was speculation that a sense of "moral outrage" drove this argument. Tony Blair stated that European powers could not stand idly by in the face of atrocity. He stated, "My generation never thought to see those scenes in Europe again."

29. Bowring, "Degradation," 14.

30. Bowring, "Degradation," 14.

31. Bowring, "Degradation," 15 (quoting Michael Byers, "Terrorism, the Use of Force and International Law after September 11th," *International and Comparative Law Quarterly* 51 (2002): 401.

32. Bowring, "Degradation," 15.

33. Thomas M. Franck, "Terrorism and the Right to Self Defence," editorial comments, *American Journal of International Law* 95 (1999): 839.

34. Bill Bowring, "Degradation," 15.

35. The attorney general's clarification for a legal basis for use of force against Iraq. Foreign and Commonwealth Office website, www.fco.gov.uk (March 18, 2003).

36. For example, Jack Straw's foreword to the Foreign and Commonwealth Office's *Annual Report on Human Rights, 2003* refers to the war against Iraq as "advancing the cause of human rights." There is, of course, a great difference between this kind of text and a legal justification for the war. The point is, however, that the justification for war is moving away from the need to prevent the use of weapons of mass destruction and moving toward a broader argument about human rights (see www.fco.gov.uk/Files/KFile/FullReport.pdf). A somewhat different approach to justification for the war is to refocus the reason for the invasion on Iraq's failure to cooperate with the UN rather than the possession of weapons of mass destruction in itself. For instance, when the Foreign Affairs Committee's *Report on the War against Terrorism* was published, Bill Rammell, Foreign and Commonwealth Office minister, argued, "By unanimously supporting UNSCR 1441 the Security Council agreed on the threat posed by Iraq and its WMD programmes. We do not accept that UN-MOVIC and IAEA had not presented any compelling evidence of WMD. But the issue was Iraq's unwillingness to co-operate and account for its WMD. Some members of the Security Council disagreed with us, not on the threat, but on how to deal with the threat. We stand by the legality of and justification for taking military action. We remain confident that the evidence of WMD and the grisly testimony of the mass graves will in time demonstrate that we made the right choice" (see www.fco.gov.uk/servlet/Front?pagename = Open Market/Xcelerate/ShowPage&c = Page&cid = 1007029391638&a = KArticle& aid = 1059132508906).

37. See Costas Douzinas, "Postmodern Just Wars," in Strawson, *Law after Ground Zero.*

38. Before the war, the UN had been active in the Oil for Food program. Under this program, oil was exported, and revenues were used to pay for humanitarian aid, although oil revenue was also used to pay for compensation and reparations for the last Gulf War and to meet the administrative and running costs of the program itself.

39. UN/World Bank, *Joint Iraq Needs Assessment* (October 2002), 11, at http://lnweb18.worldbank.org/mna/mena.nsf/Attachments/Iraq + Joint + Needs + Assessment.

40. See Iraq Donor's Conference press briefing at www.imf.org/external/np/tr/2003/tr031023.htm. See also, *Conclusions from Donors Conference* at www.comisionadoiraq.org/donors/comun/discursos/summary%20final_ing.pdf. This interconnection can be appreciated in the following brief description of the key areas of reconstruction. The Electricity Network Rehabilitation was run by the UNDP but by November 2004 will be in the hands of the Coalition Provisional Authority; the program is essential to capacity building in both industry and public services. The port of Um Qasr, essential for the movement of imports and exports, is also being dredged and upgraded with the UNDP working alongside a USAID-contracted company. The Iraq Reconstruction and Employment Program aims to employ the disadvantaged in labor-intensive reconstruction work with a focus on "basic social infrastructure repairs." See also, UN/World Bank, *Joint Needs Assessment*, 14–52.

41. The problem for the new Iraqi regime is how to appear trustworthy to the financial world at large. A further problem is that Iraq is not a signatory to the convention for settling claims through the World Bank or the International Court for the Settlement of Investment Disputes.

42. UN/World Bank, *Joint Iraq Needs Assessment*, 3.

43. UN/World Bank, *Joint Iraq Needs Assessment*, 40.

44. UN/World Bank, *Joint Iraq Needs Assessment*, 56.

45. UNDP website at www.iq.undp.org.

46. See www.undp.org/dpa/pressrelease/releases/2003/june/24jun03.html.

47. The information in this and the following paragraphs is taken from press briefings summarized in April 2003 at http://web.worldbank.org/WBSITE/EXTERNAL/NEWS/0,,cntryMDK:82603~menuPK:34466~pagePK:117705~piPK:43820~theSitePK:4607,00.html. See also, www.corpwatch.org/news/PND.jsp?articleid=8770.

48. See World Bank (note 47).

49. *International Herald Tribune*, April 3, 2003, www.iht.com/articles/91917.html. One particular issue is the control of the communications industry. It is alleged that Vodaphone has been making overtures, but the differences in telecommunications technology between Europe and the United States strongly suggest that this share of the market will be awarded to U.S. companies.

50. Jean-Luc Nancy, *Le Sens Du Monde* (Paris: Galilee, 2001); Jacques Derrida, *Voyous* (Paris: Galilee, 2003).

51. Phillipe Lacoue-Labarthe and Jean-Luc Nancy, *Retreating the Political* (London: Routledge, 1997).

52. See Costas Douzinas, *The End of Human Rights* (Oxford: Hart Press, 1999).

53. *The National Security Strategy of the United States* (September 2002), www.whitehouse.gov/nsc/nss.pdf.

"LET THE DESPICABLE ONES BE DESPISED"

The trial of Saddam represents something of an ending. However, while there are few who would not celebrate the capture of Saddam, it is difficult to see his trial as the final triumph of the war. To present the "monster" in the dock tends to individualize and personify issues of responsibility and culpability that are more complex, systemic, and institutional. At the same time, there is a need to hold an individual responsible for the appalling crimes of a regime. So, the trial of Saddam Hussein repeats an old problem. There have, of course, been other trials for war crimes and crimes against humanity. Indeed, the end of the Second World War was defined by the trials at Nuremberg (1945) and Tokyo (1946). More recently, there have been tribunals with a jurisdiction over war crimes in the former Yugoslavia (1993) and Rwanda (1994). In all these instances, the trial functions as a symbolic moment when the crimes of the past are settled and a new beginning becomes possible. However, there are always tensions that attend the birth of the new order. Those on trial might appear as the ones unlucky enough to be caught. There will always be some coherence between the old and new regimes; bureaucrats of the new regime with the task of allotting parking permits may once have signed death warrants. It is as if the justice of the law is never complete enough.

The war crimes trial also raises the problem of "victor's justice." The victors set up a court to try the vanquished. This might mean that this most necessary of symbolic moments, this desperate attempt to inaugurate a future, is compromised. Justice, which should be impartial, is seen to operate in a very partial manner: "You are guilty because you lost." These inherent tensions are intensified in the trial of Saddam Hussein.

The problem is that of hubris: Who dares speak for justice? Might those who claim the privilege find that the principles they evoke turn back on themselves? This concern can be connected to one of the closing themes of the last chapter: who can claim to speak for humanity? Once again, there is the issue of who assumes the authority to speak for all. This question of authority runs through the rhetoric of President Bush, the ideology of human rights and international law, and the certainties of religious fundamentalism. All these ideologies enable one person to claim the authority to speak for humanity: to be the one who speaks for all.

How is it possible to speak or act in the name of humanity? In whose name and by reference to which law is Saddam Hussein to be tried?

This question would appear distasteful to those who have survived the regime. Saddam must answer for his crimes against the Iraqi people.[1] But if the judgment and punishment of Saddam Hussein is to be more than revenge for the atrocities of the past, if it is necessary to invoke the justice of the law, how is this law to be composed? How is this justice to be realized?

What is at stake may already have emerged when Saddam first appeared before the court set up by the Provisional Authority.* Saddam was placed in front of an Iraqi judge. This preliminary encounter between the former president and the court concerned the issue of who could judge and who could accuse.

The judge demanded that Saddam confirm his identity. Saddam

---

*On July 1, 2004, Saddam Hussein was arraigned before a court set up by the Coalition Provisional Authority in December 2003. This hearing took place after the transfer of sovereignty from the CPA to the interim Iraqi government on June 30, 2004.

turned the question back on the judge: What allowed the judge to ask such a question? The judge answered: "I am a representative of the criminal courts of Iraq." But what founds or justifies this law? This was indeed the substance of Saddam's riposte. The new Iraq is no more than a creation of an invading force, an illegitimate regime. Saddam stated that he himself represents Iraq. He lives "in the heart of every Iraqi." Saddam is a people, a history, and a place. Destiny personified.

How can Saddam be judged? The International Criminal Court might have tried Saddam, but as yet it does not have jurisdiction.[2] If one asserts that the new Iraqi courts have the jurisdiction to try Saddam by virtue of being the de facto power, one runs the risk of merely confirming the suspicion of victor's justice. Simply asserting that "might is right" is a weak argument in this context precisely because what is at stake is the legitimacy of the new regime.

For the international community, a legitimate trial must be founded on principles drawn from international law. These principles determine the substantive charges against Saddam, the other members of the former regime, and the actual procedure of the trial itself. The crimes of the former regime can be tried by reference to humanitarian law and the law of war.[3]

Comparing the situation in Iraq to that in other "post"-conflict societies such as Rwanda and the former Yugoslavia, some have argued that the tribunal for Saddam's trial should be set up by a resolution of the UN Security Council. This tribunal would then be charged with coordinating efforts to preserve evidence and with establishing minimum standards for evidence. A UN tribunal would also interact with the existing structure of criminal courts to ensure that only the international tribunal dealt with those charged with the most heinous offenses. It would also establish requirements for truth and reconciliation mechanisms to deal with the kind of claims and cases that were not suitable for criminal courts.

Immediately there are problems. The Iraqi response to the international community stresses the need to "deal with" criminals by reference to Iraqi law. Some commentators have also suggested that there is a hostility or a reluctance to work with the UN. Rather than resolve the issue of locality or universality, this issue merely relocates the debate. As Iraqi law is based on an Egyptian version of the French code, it takes us back to the issue of the transferability or translatability of suppos-edly universal principles.

If it were possible, then, to determine a principle of humanity in whose name the tyrant is judged, it would have to appear in the trial of Saddam Hussein. In judging, the judge speaks the law: the judge articu-lates and applies a principle. In the case of war crimes and crimes against humanity, the principle represents a value that is common to humanity.[4] In that sense the judge becomes a representative of those in whose names the principle has been articulated, the victims of atrocit-ies. When a judge speaks for a principle, in the moment of judgment, the judge invokes the principle and speaks for the victims. In this sense the judge effaces his- or herself and speaks for a principle that applies universally. The tyrant, who claims to be able to speak for everyone, is judged in the name of all those who cannot make themselves present, for whom the judge must speak. In so speaking, in the moment of judg-ment, the judge must become a no one, no one who can thus speak for everyone.

Might this be the way that humanity announces itself? Perhaps hu-manity demands that no one speaks for us all.

Notes

1. Local Iraqi judges have been collecting evidence and initiating prosecu-tions. The murders of Muhan Jabr al-Shuwaili, an al-Najaf governorate judge, and Isma'il Yusif Sadiq, a judge from Mosul in November 2004, suggest just what is at stake in these claims for justice. An example of another local initia-tive would be that of the Association of Victims in Basra, who are building up an archive, preserving documents and evidence that relate to atrocities com-mitted by the old regime.

2. Set up by the Rome Statute of the International Criminal Court, the court will have jurisdiction over "the most serious crimes of concern to the interna-tional community as a whole." The Rome Statute lists these serious crimes as genocide, crimes against humanity, war crimes, and the crime of aggression. At present the United States is not a signatory to the Rome Statute, and thus American citizens will not be subject to its jurisdiction. The United States has argued that the court will be manipulated to enable politically motivated actions to be brought against Americans. As American citizens are still bound by the Geneva and Hague conventions, this should not be seen as an argument

that Americans are somehow exempt from responsibility for such crimes. Amnesty International has, however, called the refusal of the United States to sign the statute "a threat to the international system of justice" and has argued that there are strong safeguards against politically motivated prosecutions. See www.amnestyusa.org/news/2002/world07012002.html. It would appear that UN-sanctioned exemptions for U.S. service personnel are now a precondition of U.S. involvement in peacekeeping. See www.hrw.org/campaigns/icc/us.htm.

Should Saddam be tried by the International Criminal Court (ICC)? As neither Iraq nor the United States has accepted the jurisdiction of the ICC, the court has no power to investigate or prosecute war crimes or crimes against humanity committed either by an American or an Iraqi citizen. For Saddam and other regime members to be tried by the ICC, there would have to be a recommendation of the UN Security Council, but this is unlikely to occur without American support. The fact that the jurisdiction extends only over crimes committed after July 1, 2002, would also make it a somewhat limited forum for the trial of Saddam and other regime members.

It would appear that Saddam remains in a form of legal limbo. The date set for his trial is now the beginning of 2006. According to Iraq's national security advisor, Mouwafak al Rubaie, "this is going to be probably the trial of the century, and we have to get it right" (*Miami Herald*, December 13, 2004).

3. The definition of *crimes against humanity* comes from the principles of the Nuremberg Tribunal of 1950. Principle 6 defines three crimes under international law: crimes against the peace, war crimes, and crimes against humanity. Crimes against the peace include the preparation or waging of a war of "aggression" or a "war in violation of international treaties." War crimes are crimes against the laws and customs of war. The definition of the crime covers mistreatment and murder of civilians as well as prisoners of war; it also covers the "wanton destruction" of property. Crimes against humanity are "murder, extermination, enslavement, deportation and other inhuman acts done against any civilian population, or persecutions on political, racial or religious grounds, when such acts are done or such persecutions are carried on in execution of or in connection with any crime against peace or any war crime."

4. The problem of who can speak for everyone is at its most acute in international humanitarian law, the law of war, and international criminal law, as these bodies of law tend to separate themselves from the old founding notions of sovereignty. Humanitarian law has to move beyond the founding fiction of sovereignty and ground itself by reference to "humanity" as a whole.

INDEX

law: as communication, 10; economics and, 11–12, 38–39, 90; globalization and, 5, 9–15; hard, 18–19, 60; justice and, 54–55; positivism and, 42; power and, 11–13; soft, 18–19, 60, 81–82n2; sovereignty and, 9–11, 27n34
law of war, 21
least-developed countries, 82n4
Lefebvre, Henri, 31n67, 59
legal imperialism, 11–12
Lesotho Highland Water Project, 105
lex mercatoria, 9–10
loans: IMF and, 63–66, 84n28; international system of, 106–7; World Bank and, 66–69
local politics: general interest versus, 49; Ogoni people and, 48–49
Lowenfeld, Andreas F., 11, 29n51, 65, 69

MacMillan, Fiona, 11
Mann, F. A., 62
Marshall, James, 44
Marx, Karl: and French Revolution, 26n30; and social power, 13
Mcintyre, Ben, 115
mercantilism, 6
military intervention, 14–15, 21–22, 116–25, 135n6. See also law of war; use of force
military regimes, 93
modernization theory, 90–93
monetary system, international, 83n5
Most Favored Nation provision, 72, 75–76
multilateral agreements: number of, 4; WTO and, 78
Multilateral Investment Agreement, 79

national treatment provisions, 72
nations: formation of, 34; role of, 16
NATO (North Atlantic Treaty Organization), 122–24
negotiations, GATT and, 71–72, 75–76
Negri, A., 12, 13
new international economic order (NIEO): development law and, 90,

94–96, 98; failure of, 20; and sovereignty, 99
Nicaragua, 68
NIEO. See new international economic order
Nigeria, 33–55; Britain and, 34–39, 42–44, 46; constitution of, 35–36, 39; corruption in, 47–48; economics of, 37–41; ethnicities in, 36–37, 45; formation of, 34–35; jurisprudence in, 41–45; and Ogoni people, 45–54; oil in, 37, 38–39, 47–48

Obasanjo, Olusegun, 42
Ogoni people: Bill of Rights of, 18, 48–49; history of, 45–46; injustices against, 51–54; and oil, 47–48; political claims of, 46–47, 49; riot and executions, 49–51
oil, in Nigeria, 37, 38–39, 47
Ojukwu, Chukwuemeka Odumegwu, 37
Olawoyin v. Commissioner of Police, 44
Oppenheim's International Law, 117

Pakistan, 66
Perez de Cuellar, Javier, 117
plurilateral agreements, 78
positivism in law, 42, 118
Poverty Reduction and Growth Facility, 66
power: law and, 11–13; sovereignty and, 13
problematic, definition of, 29n56
proportionality principle, 118
Proposals for Expansion of World Trade and Employment, 69
protectionism, 6
public services, 104

Quereshi, Asif, 29n51

Raffer, Kunibert, 106
recession, 3–4
reconstruction of Iraq, 125–30
regime theory, 10
regulation, 81n2
relief agencies, 135n6

ABOUT THE AUTHOR

Adam Gearey is a senior lecturer in law at Birkbeck College, University of London. He is a member of the central committee of the critical legal conference and author of *Law and Aesthetics* (1999) and, most recently, "Love and Death in American Jurisprudence"(2004).